EUROPE'S
Castle
and Palace
Hotels

CAROLE CHESTER

CHRISTOPHER HELM

London

© 1989 Carole Chester
Line illustrations by Isabel Lovering
Maps by Graham Douglas
Christopher Helm (Publishers) Ltd, Imperial House,
21–25 North Street, Bromley, Kent BR1 1SD

ISBN 0-7470-0415-3 (UK)

A CIP catalogue record for this book
is available from the British Library

First published in North America by
Hunter Publishing Inc.
300 Raritan Center Parkway
CN 94, Edison, N.J. 08818, USA
Tel. 201 225 1900

ISBN 1-55650-171-4 (US)

Typeset by Tradespools Ltd, Frome, Somerset
Printed and bound in Spain.
by Gráficas Estella, S.A. Navarra.

Contents

Key to Symbols

Information is given on each hotel concerning the facilities, situation, price, and so on. The following system of symbols has been used:

| 3 | Number of rooms

🏠 Opening dates
✗ Cuisine
✳ Ambience
ℐ Recreation
♫ Entertainment
£/$ Price (Graded from A —
the most expensive — to E)

INTRODUCTION

Europe is quite justifiably renowned for its myriad castles and palaces, but only in fairly recent years have so many of them taken on a new lease of life — as hotels. Some are small, some large, some have added extensions. Some are state owned, some are family owned. By accepting paying guests, many have been saved from neglect, their history visibly preserved.

This book contains a selection of what, in my opinion, are the best and most historic places to stay in in countries that are easily visited. The choice has been made from personal knowledge and that of respected colleagues — none of the hotels mentioned has paid for inclusion. Although historic links are priority, I have obviously taken cuisine, ambience and service into consideration. Although I admit to slightly 'cheating' in one or two cases, almost all the hotels written about have been true castles or palaces in the past.

Chefs and owners (not to mention prices) do of course change as quickly as newly converted properties come on stream. If there is a castle or palace hotel you know about, that is not listed here, or indeed one you think should be omitted, please let me know, via the publishers. Comments and recommendations for future issues of this book will be gratefully appreciated.

In the meantime, don't just dream of living like a lord — discover the places where you can do so.

FRANCE

Many of Europe's finest castle hotels are located in France. Generally speaking they are not terribly large and are often privately owned, though they may be members of a consortium. One of the best consortiums is Relais et Châteaux (which has representation in the US) — a number of their members are included here. In addition to the historic element, the hotels are noted for their exceptional cuisine and comfort and a high standard of service. They tend to be in the luxury bracket, both in price and style, offering beautifully presented food that will be appreciated by the gourmet. The consortium was the result of a merger between Châteaux-Hotels of France, of which René Traversac was president and founder, and Relais de Campagne — a group of hotels best known for their peaceful rural settings.

There are several other French consortia whose members include former castles, convents or palatial manors: Châteaux Hôtels Indépendants is one to look out for where the hotels are independently owned, offer reasonably good facilities and plenty of atmosphere. Châteaux d'Accueil is another with privately owned hotels, but these tend to be smaller, more simple and less expensive. Relais du Silence is a third where owners have decided to accept a few paying guests in order to maintain their properties.

French castle hotel owners are frequently titled, though they may well have hired a manager to run their establishments efficiently. Conversions have come about from necessity either because an estate was on the verge of bankruptcy or in need of repair and maintenance.

L'Abbaye Saint-Michel

Near the castles of Burgundy stands this super and ancient abbey hotel, brimming with history. We know that Count of Tonnerre Miles I founded an abbey on this site in 898 and that Saint-Thiery, who died in 1022, was buried here. From the 11th to the 17th century the abbey was the most important religious establishment in the region, welcoming, among others, Joan of Arc in 1429 on her way to Chinon.

Though the abbey lost its splendid decorations and relics in the 18th century, when it was dismantled, the remnants have been incorporated into an interesting luxury hotel. The old stonework has become the basis of the lobby, the vaulted cellars, an atmospheric dining room and there are tennis courts in the old abbey garden.

89700 Tonnerre (Yonne), France. ℘ (86) 55 05 99

16	(including suites; all with en suite bathroom, TV and refrigerator-bar)	✳	Unique and quiet
	mid Feb–Dec	♪	Tennis
✕	Relais gourmand standard with reputable cellar. Restaurant is closed Mon and Tue, Feb–Apr, Sep–Dec	♪	No
		£/$	B

Château d'Artigny

Draw up in front of d'Artigny and you could be forgiven for thinking you'd arrived at Versailles: the façade is imposing, palatial, the grounds, manicured and full of flowers. Yet d'Artigny has never been a palace in the historic sense, albeit an 11th-century fortress once stood on this site, replaced by an elegant château in 1769. The latter survived the Revolution intact to become the property of several aristocratic families, like Les Lambron de Maudox and Les Gaillet de Boufferie. But it is best known for having been François Coty's home. Coty, who purchased the place in 1912, demolished the original château and had a new one purpose-built to his own dream design in 18th-century style. It was industrial intrepreneur, René Traversac, who acquired the château in 1959 and converted it into the luxury hotel it is today.

There's no doubt about it — this château does look very grand from the moment you walk into the hall to the moment you climb the Lens stone staircase. What used to be Coty's library has become an enormous lounge bar, complete with piano. The marble floor of the large dining room is encrusted with gilded bronze; the smaller second dining room is circular with ornate columns. Delicate panelling decorates the Regency Ballroom and, on the first floor, is a rotunda whose ceiling is decorated with a magnificent *trompe-l'œil* fresco. This work of Hoffbauer portrays Coty's friends and parents at a masked ball at the château.

Guests don't have to use all the rooms to look around. On the second floor, for example, the white marble former kitchen once adjoined the pink and green marble patisserie. A large split-level, mosaiced-floor cloakroom was once linked to the main suite by way of a secret staircase, and comprises 78 inlaid wooden cupboards. In the main courtyard (but linked by covered walkway), Ariane's Pavilion was built as a replica of the Royal Chapel at Versailles and now houses guest suites. Bedrooms, all sumptuously furnished, are to be found in the main château itself, this pavilion, the hunting pavilion and the Port-Moulin pavilion on the banks of the Indre River. With the château's background in mind, all the meeting rooms are named for elements of perfume.

D'Artigny is favoured by conference groups but, thanks to its size and spacious grounds, individuals won't feel left out. There is a heated outdoor pool, bowling green and putting green plus two tennis courts. Food, as one would hope, is excellent, complemented by a particularly fine wine cellar which holds 45,000 bottles of all the best French vintages since 1918.

The hotel is a perfect base for touring the Loire Valley, well noted for its historic châteaux. Son et Lumière performances are given at the one at Azay-le-Rideau, 20 km (12 miles) away and also at Amboise, 37 km (23 miles) away, Villandry (34 km, 21 miles), Loches (33 km, 20½ miles) and Chambord (60 km, 37 miles). D'Artigny is located a mere 15 km (9 miles) from Tours.

Route d'Azay-le-Rideau, 37250 Veigne-Montbazon (Indre-et-Loire), France. ✆ (47) 26 24 24

55	(mostly double and suites, including duplexes, the majority in the main house; all with en suite bathrooms)	✳ Grandiose luxury
🏨	mid Jan–Nov	℘ Outdoor pool, heated Apr–Oct. Two tennis courts, putting green, bowling green; signposted walks. 18-hole golf course a 15-minute drive away, horse riding 30 minutes away. Fishing is available at Port Moulin. Hot-air balloon flights
✕	Regional specialities, short and seasonal menus. Excellent wine list and fine old ports and brandies	
		♫ Musical evenings, poolside barbecues. Piano music in the lounge bar
		£/$ A

Hôtel de l'Aigle Noir

This old distinguished building faces the gardens of Napoléon's favourite palace and its grand style is very much in keeping with Fontainebleau. The hotel is not offputtingly snobby — you'll find a warm welcome and cheerful atmosphere. Service is attentive in the 18th-century-styled dining room whose cuisine has won top awards. There is also a more casual restaurant.

Empire-style guest rooms in jewel colours have all modern conveniences, some discreetly tucked away, and an interesting set of prints decorate the walls of the reception rooms. Essentially a gracious overnight stop only 45 minutes from Paris suited to visitors intent on exploring Fontainebleau thoroughly.

27 place Napoléon Bonaparte, Fontainebleau, (Seine et Marne), France. ℘ (64) 22 32 65

30	(including suites, all individually decorated; all with private bathroom, colour TV and mini bar)	✳	Regal, but not stuffy
		℘	No, but two small gardens and the château park is near. Riding 7 km (4 miles)
🏠	Year round	♫	No
✕	Traditional French cuisine in both the Beauharnais and the Bivouac restaurants	£/$	B

Château d'Audrieu

Of an evening, Château d'Audrieu is deceptively hard to find; by morning's light it is incredibly close to Caen. This is the beauty of this very fine family home. Surrounded as it is by a patchwork of tree-bordered fields and farms and flower-filled gardens, its entrance reached via a magnificent drive, it gives the impression of being in the middle of nowhere, yet in actuality it is a very short distance from Bayeaux.

The present proprietor, Gerard Livry-Level, played and ate here as a child. Then, the upstairs private dining room was the family dining room, today's bar, the saddle room, and what are now comfortable guest rooms were stables and hay lofts. The building as you see it today, very much the private château, flanking three-quarters of a courtyard, dates from the 18th century but its history extends well beyond that.

It is said that the first ruler of these lands was Lord Percy, personal chef to William the Conqueror. Legend would have you believe that he killed a Saxon or two with a colander spoon, for which feat he was dubbed a baron. Fact or fiction, the first Lord Percy certainly established himself in England while retaining his French property — he founded the nearby Abbey of Juaye-Mondaye, for example.

Of the two branches of the Percy family, those remaining in Normandy replaced the original modest feudal residence with a proper castle in the 15th century, remnants of which have been incorporated in Audrieu as it is now. The line died out when Marguerite married Guillaume de Seran in 1593, after which it passed from Seran to Seran until Camille Leonor — who managed to recover his property after the French Revolution, despite its confiscation, and will it to his daughter, Henriette, through whom in direct line it has descended to its present owners.

As a hotel, the château is a welcoming, elegant establishment — not too formal, yet not jeans-casual — whose staff speak good English and whose amenities are reminiscent of an English stately home. There are antiques at Audrieu but you 'happen' upon them — fine old wooden pieces — in the corridors and upstairs lounges. The bar (and it is a bar) is minuscule so most people take an apéritif in the pastel-decor drawing room. The guest rooms don't have American-style standup showers or radios, but the soap is Jean Patou. The pretty dining room (split into two for intimacy) features overhead chandeliers, table lights or candles and optimum service — for à la carte selections or the gourmet table d'hôte. The cuisine is not typical of Normandy though the dishes are based on local produce and everything is made to order.

Château d'Audrieu's location is, of course, close to the Normandy Beaches. Indeed, it was nearly destroyed at the time of the 1944 Landings for it was in the no man's land between enemy lines, repeatedly attacked by British and Canadians from one side, and by a German Panzer division from the other. It was hit by 27 105 mm shells but Caen stone proved the tougher and stood up to the punishment. Caen airport is 15 km (9 miles) away.

14250 Tilly-sur-Seulles (Calvados), France.
✆ (31) 80 21 52

21	(No. 12 is the only single room; all others twins or suites; all with en suite bathroom)	✳	Stylish country château
		℘	Swimming pool, tennis. Hot-air ballooning available
▥	Mar–Dec	♫	No
✕	Deliciously nouvelle French, e.g. warm lobster salad, followed by lamb and a side dish of potatoes cooked with leeks and cream, then apple tart with caramel sauce. Always a complimentary hors d'œuvre (dégustation)	£/$	B

Château d'Ayres

Three times a monastery, this pleasant château is a recommended stopover between the gorges of the River Tarn and the River Jute. The very first 7th-century monastery erected here was destroyed by the Sarazin invasion and the 8th-century priory of Ayres was destroyed during the Aquitaine wars. Then in 1025 a monk named Martin created a large domain that became known as Saint Martin of Ayres.

When the Protestants became too strong in this Cevenol land, the monks left in the 16th century and a Protestant family, the Galtiers of Montauran, remodelled it into a private home. As retribution for the courtesies offered to the Duke of Rohan's protestant troops, Cardinal Richelieu ordered the château to be demolished and it lost its towers.

The de Nogaret family reconstructed d'Ayres in the 18th century. The castle survived the French Revolution and was sold at the beginning of the 20th century to be turned into a country inn.

48150 Meyrueis (Gorges du Tarn), France.
☎ (66) 45 60 10

20	(all with private bathroom)	✳	Peace with character
		⚲	Tennis. Country walks
🏛	Apr–mid Oct	♫	No
✕	Traditional French	£/$	C

Château de Bassignac

This private castle was built in the 16th century replacing a manor of far earlier origins, which was also in the Bassignac family hands. One of the most memorable occasions was the Grand Condé's stay here in 1652 when a political set-to took place between the Comte de Bassignac and the Prince, who was travelling incognito. Records mention the occasion but all the furniture from the period has disappeared save for one piece of earthenware in the large salon. There is, however, a well-preserved stone carved coat of arms of the d'Anglars de Bassignac family on the staircase.

From today's guests' point of view, there is the opportunity to fish on the property, visit the medieval city of Salers and the Roman churches and castles of the High Auvergne.

Bassignac, 15240 Saignes (Cantal), France.
✆ (71) 40 82 82

4	(double or twin. Rates include breakfast)	✳	Private home appeal
		℘	Fishing in the grounds.
🏨	Easter–Nov		Tennis and swimming
✗	Dinner is available with		nearby
	advance notice — a set	♫	No
	price menu includes	£/$	C
	apéritif and wine		

Château de Bellinglise

The panache of a four-star hotel; the building of 16th-century design. The Château Bellinglise has both though in actual fact it is built on 13th-century foundations, and during 19th-century excavations a number of Roman tiles and sarcophagi were discovered. A manor house at Elincourt was first mentioned in 1348, owned by the Hamel family. Enlarged in 1476, the château was used as a court of justice with a prison in one of the towers, it now known as the clock tower. Between the 17th and 20th centuries, the castle belonged to several different titled families.

New décor has given the interior of Bellinglise glamour: a dining room that features velvet, silk and wood panelling, lit by crystal chandeliers; a fresh and airy breakfast room — the winter garden — that opens on to greenery; luxurious bedrooms in the main building or the conference centre.

60157 Elincourt-Ste-Marguerite (Oise), France.
✆ (44) 76 04 76

47	(doubles, including some suites; all with en suite bathroom, colour TV, and mini bar)	✳	Glamorous four star hotel
		♆	Billiard room, tennis court, horse riding, swimming pool, 18-hole golf course
🏨	Year round	♫	No
✕	Quality traditional French	£/$	B

Château de Berchères

In the old days the owners of this country home were shepherds — in the 12th century the village in which it is situated was called Bergière, then Berchière, from the word 'berger' (shepherd). It became a stronghold of the Canons of Chartres in the 15th century so that, when the Richebourg family settled here, it was a turreted castle.

One of its many owners was Vailard, a family well known to political and religious circles. Louis Colbert was another, but when Monsieur de Beaumanoir purchased it in 1760, he decided to have the château rebuilt in the style then in vogue and called in Louis XV's architect, Antoine, to do so.

Restored and decorated in deep pinks, blues and reds, the château's 32 guest bedrooms have all been modernised. Its public rooms are in keeping with its stately manor image and its setting, a gem of greenery with a lake in front of the hotel and the River Vesgre that winds through the park where rare old trees are planted.

28560 Berchères-sur-Vesgre (Ile de France), France.
✆ (37) 82 07 21

32	(all with en suite bathroom)	✳	Calm manor house
		℘	Tennis
▥	Jan–Jul, Sep–24 Dec	♫	No
✕	Traditional French	£/$	C

Château des Blosses

This fascinating small château was built by the current owners' great grandfather on the estate of Rouërie, land that straddles the Normandy/Brittany border. The La Rouërie family name is an old and noble one, whose descendants were royal supporters, which is not to say the last of the line, Marquis Armand de la Rouërie, did not go off to America to join their revolution in 1777. His American comrades knew him as Colonel Armand and he was awarded the Cross of Cincinnatus by George Washington, himself.

The American Revolution was one thing, but when the Marquis returned to France to find his own country torn by revolt, his own heart was with the monarchy and he became one of the founders of the main counter-revolutionary group, 'La Chouannerie'. The name stems from the French word for owl, 'chouette', for the owl's 'cry' was used by the royalists as their night-time signals as well as their battle cry. Much of the fighting took place around Rouerie and many of those who live here today refer to their ancestors as 'the owls'.

When Louis XVIII died and was succeeded in 1824 by his brother, Charles X, it was the Barbier family who bought the Rouerie estate and its old château and, in 1888, erected the newer property where you can stay today. The name

'Blosses' refers to the white cherry tree blossoms in the grounds.

Monsieur and Madame Barbier have given a name to each of their five guest rooms and include what they call a 'greedy breakfast' for the overnight rate. They have also added a 9-hole practice golf area in the grounds.

35460 Saint-Ouen-Rouerie (Ille-et-Vilaine), France.
✆ **(99) 98 36 16**

5	(all double or twin, all individually named and decorated; all with en suite bathroom)	✳	Peaceful
🏛	Feb–mid Nov	♪	No, but nearby tennis courts, riding 12 km (7½ miles), pool 25 km (15½ miles)
✗	Table d'hôte on request	♫	No
		£/$	C

Château de Brecourt

It would be hard to find a prettier-looking château than Brecourt, built in typical Louis XIII style of stone with pink brick panels and gabled slate roof. Overlooking its own park and fields, Brecourt's origins are 17th and 18th century. Jean Jubert-Sire (whose family had owned the land since 1531) built the first residence here in 1625, a property which remained in the family's hands until 1706 when it passed to the Counts of Monçeau and then to the Guesdier de Saint-Aubin family. From 1930 to 1939, it was the home of Norman Armour, US Ambassador to France.

Post-war restoration gave the château new and revived life without losing any of its previous distinguished air, as you will find when you sit in the large Salle d'Armes on the ground floor, with its polished black marble flagstones and its Louis XIII fireplace, not to mention its dark wood panelling and beamed ceiling.

The beautifully carved staircase banister rail dates to when the château was first built, and what is now the dining room on the first floor is also decorated with old woodwork, and a 17th-century open fireplace. Brecourt isn't large but it seems to be so with its many corridors and flights of stairs to reach guest rooms, all individually styled and sized.

It has only been a hotel since 1981 and has since recently converted one of the outhouses that faces the courtyard into an indoor pool and jacuzzi area. Reached in less than an hour from Paris, this is a splendidly quiet base for overnighting on the way in or out of Normandy.

Douains, 27120 Pacy-sur-Eure (Eure), France.
✆ (32) 52 40 50

20		✳	Atmospheric castle
🏨	Year round	℘	Indoor pool and jacuzzi. Tennis
✕	Typical Relais including unusual 18th-century dishes, e.g. pigeon marinaded in lemon	♫	No
		£/$	B

Château de Brindos

Brindos reminds most people of a rather grand parador. Well, it is located in the heart of Basque country so Spain is very near, and it does boast a tall fireplace from Toledo that dates from the Middle Ages. But it is French despite the fact the present building was created by an Englishman (Reginald Wright) and an American (Virginia Gould), for local archives tell of a Brindos castle during the 15th century.

In 1952, the Wrights' valuable collection, which had been carefully concealed during the war, went on sale and attracted antique dealers from around the world. The castle estate, having been parcelled out and abandoned, only saw new life in 1968 when the Vivensangs became proprietors of the castle, its lake and some of the wooded acreage. Repair was essential but this native-born couple, who were also from a hotel family, planned to make Brindos flourish once again, even if only a little of the former riches remained.

64600 Anglet-Biarritz (Côte Basque), France.
✆ (59) 23 17 68

15	(all with en suite bathroom)	✳	Parador-style
		℘	Swimming pool, tennis court
🏨	Year round		
✗	Standard Relais	♫	No
		£/$	B

Le Castel

Gracious looking le Castel has been in Baronne de Ville d'Avray's family for 100 years, but it was built in 1760 in the reign of Louis XV. At that time the parliament of Normandy was sitting in Bayeux and the owner of the property was the Chevalier Freard du Castel.

Situated in a 1.2-hectare (3-acre) country estate, this private town house is within easy reach of the D Day Beaches (though it was not damaged during World War II), and within an hour's drive of Caen, Mont Saint-Michel and Honfleur.

Three guest rooms are named for colours and a fourth is suitable for children (under the eaves). In addition, a two bedroom apartment with fully equipped kitchen and living room is available for self-caterers.

7 rue de la Cambette, 14400 Bayeux (Calvados), France. ∅ (31) 92 05 86

5	(including an apartment suited to 4 people; all with en suite bathroom. Rates include breakfast)	✳	Quiet
		℘	No, but tennis, riding, swimming and golf are all nearby and the Beaches are only 13 km (8 miles)
🏠	Easter–Nov		
✗	Dinner not available	♫	No
		£/$	C

Château de Castel Novel

It may be difficult to decide whether this château is a honeymoonish retreat or a sizeable holiday hotel since it appears to be both. It is a handsome castle for sure with its slate-roofed turrets and towers and its rosy stone façade to which ivy clings. Equally assured is the fact it was once a fortress in a strategic position — sheer rock face to the north, open ground to the south. The most visible sign of that era is the solid circular tower built with rough-hewn stones. The corner tower would have been the keep, serving as a lookout post. Much of the castle dates from the 14th century though it has since been renovated, but excavations around its foundations have unearthed Roman coins. The first mention of a castle was in a 1289 document when it was associated with the family of Pida of Castel Novel. In 1316, the name reappears when Guichard de Comborn gifted it to the Squire of Pompadour.

In 1440, a successor of the Camborn family, Jean de Bretagne, Vicomte de Limoges, gave this outpost of the County of Limoges to his equerry, Jean Beaupoil, as a wedding present for use during his lifetime, and the gift was completed by the 1441 sale of the manor house of Castel Novel for 2000 gold crowns. Towards the end of 1500, Françoise de Beaupoil married Gilles d'Aubusson, so for the next three centuries the castle belonged to that famous family.

In 1844, Alexandre Lambert, Vicomte d'Aubusson de la Feuillade sold the land and château to Baron Jacques-Leon de Jouvenel who died there in 1886. A more familiar name to us was one of the last owners before Castel Novel became a hotel — that of Colette, who wrote several novels here. Her room is now the Louis XVI suite. All the rooms are completely different, some rustic, some modern. Among the most interesting is the round Louis XIII room in the large tower and also the duplex in the small tower where wooden stairs lead to a child's room. Some of the rooms are in a newer building not far from the main château where you can expect Laura Ashley-style wallpaper with matching drapes and bedspreads.

There is a choice of three restaurants: one in the form of a covered terrace with country-style furnishings and a view of the gardens; another, Louis XIII with a large feature fireplace; and the third with a magnificent painted ceiling. A rosette for the menu supports the concept that food here is some of the best in Périgord.

That 'holiday' element comes from the grounds and their large swimming pool, tennis court, driving range and footpaths. The hillside location above the Vézère gorges and the château Pompadour is a good one for visiting Sarlat, the caves of Lascaux and Rocamadour. Brive airport is 5 km (3 miles) away.

Route d'Objat—D901, 19240 Varetz (Corrèze), France.
✆ (55) 85 00 01

38	(mostly in the main house, including suites, all individually decorated, some historic, some with canopied beds; all with en suite bathroom)	✳	Raffine but not rigid
		℘	Swimming pool, tennis court, putting range, footpaths for walking. Horse riding nearby
🏨	May–mid Oct	♫	No
✕	Mouthwatering Périgord specialities that have won awards, served in character dining rooms	£/$	B

Hostellerie du Château

The hostellerie, an imposing conglomeration of towers and bricks, was built in the 16th century in Renaissance style and is close to the medieval ruins of a 13th-century fortified castle constructed by Louis VI's grandson. That castle was given to the Connetable of Montmorency in 1530 by François I's mother, but was confiscated by the Crown after the punishment of Henry of Montmorency in Toulouse in 1632. Later, it was returned to Charlotte of Montmorency, Prince of Condé's wife, passing through the hands of the Condé family to Philippe Egalite who demolished most of it and auctioned the furnishings in Paris.

The ruins may be reached via a Renaissance bridge and the rooms of the hotel look on to a sizeable park that includes formal lawns and gardens. Public and guest rooms are decorated in traditional French fashion.

02130 Fere-en-Tardenois (Aisne), France.
✆ (23) 82 21 13

23	(doubles and suites; all with private bathroom, TV, some with refrigerator)	✳	Formal
		⚲	Tennis court in the grounds. Fishing and riding 5 km (3 miles) away
🏨	Mar–Dec		
✕	Delicate nouvelle cuisine	♫	No
		£/$	B

Château de la Chèvre d'Or

Situated between Nice and Monte-Carlo, the Chèvre d'Or may seem remote perched as it is on the rocky pinnacle of Eze-Village, but it is in fact easily accessible, only 12 km (7½ miles) from Nice airport. The original castle dates from the 11th century, its ruins discovered by American violinist, Balakovic, and his wife in 1924 when they were climbing the slopes of Eze-Village seeking a good vantage point. What they saw first was a small goat outlined against the sky, which appeared gold in the last rays of the sun. They followed the animal, found the ruined castle and named it as you see — 'the golden goat'.

Now, years later it has become a hotel of distinction still with its superb view over the Mediterranean which guests can enjoy from a poolside chair. Decorated in a mixture of medieval and Provence style, this castle is a hideaway oasis of calm. Very small but very prestigious.

06360 Eze-Village (Moyenne Corniche), France
⌀ **(93) 41 12 12**

8	(including suites; all with en suite bathroom)	✳	Intimately romantic.
		℘	Small outdoor pool.
🏨	Mar–Nov		Tennis and golf nearby
✕	Grand French	♫	No
		£/$	A

Château de Chissay

Travel between Montrichard and Chenonceaux and you will come across a magnificent park and the towered château of Chissay. That largest tower is the oldest (11th century), two other round ones remain from Renaissance times as does the courtyard and Italian-style portico.

Chissay was established as a Seigniory in 1444 and passed from noble hand to noble hand until Antoine Ruze founded the Hospice of Montrichard here for Chissay's poor in 1714 and later was again transferred from titled family to family.

Today, the old cellars have become reception rooms, the bedrooms have mosaiced bathrooms and dining is by candle-light in the restaurant. There is a heated pool in the grounds. Chissay is located 4 km (2½ miles) from Montrichard and 40 km (25 miles) from Tours airport.

41400 Chissay-en-Touraine, Montrichard (Val de Loire), France. ✆ (54) 32 32 01

27	(all with en suite bathroom)	✳	Grand comfort
		♂	Heated outdoor pool.
🏨	Mar–Dec		Tennis, fishing and riding
✗	Specialities include sliced	♫	Musical evenings
	salmon in barbecue sauce,	£/$	B
	and stuffed pigeon		

Le Choiseul

Recent guests at charming le Choiseul have included Queen Beatrix, the US Ambassador and the Comte de Paris. Le Choiseul only recently became a hotel (opened in 1985), converted from a stately villa built for the Duke of Choiseul. It stands in the shadow of Amboise Castle, by the banks of the Loire. Big picture windows in the first floor sunny dining room overlook the river, and the door at the back opens directly on to the gardens where meals are served in summer.

The hotel looks a little Italianate with its chandeliers, mirrors and pastel colour schemes — lots of pinks and blues. The bar is more of a drawing room and guest accommodation is spread between the main house and garden pavilions. The terraced gardens, adorned by stone urns and the statuary, were actually designed in the 15th century and the addition of a modern swimming pool here hasn't detracted from the overall effect one bit.

This site was a strategic one where Caesar's Roman legions were ordered to dig great cellars into the cliffs for storing grain. You can see them still — management hopes eventually to restore them suitably into 'party' rooms.

We consider this château hotel quite a find in this city where François I lived and Leonardo da Vinci spent some years.

36 quai Charles-Guinot, 37400 Amboise (Indre et Loire), France. ✆ (47) 30 45 45

23 (doubles and suites with feminine furnishings; all with en suite bathroom)

▥ Apr–mid Jan

✕ Sandre de Loire is the speciality, but all food beautifully prepared and presented, accompanied by Touraine wines like Chinon, Bourgeuil, Vouvray and Gamay

✳ Refined and intimate

♪ Outdoor pool

♫ No

£/$ B

Château Hôtel de Coatguelen

Owned by a marquis, Coatguelen was built for his great grandfather as a summer residence in 1850. (The original Boisgelin family manor is also located in the hotel's large park and dates to the 15th century.) Furnished with a simple elegance, this château's major assets are its cuisine and its sport facilities.

Chef Louis Le Roy refers to his cooking as 'Cuisine Allegée', light but not nouvelle and gives cookery demonstrations in his kitchens several days a week for classes of 4–12 people. Though instruction is in French, an English translator is also in attendance and at the end of the demonstration (based on a complete menu), participants sample the dishes for lunch in the dining room.

Plehedel, 22290 Lanvollon (Côtes-du-Nord), France.
☎ (96) 22 31 24

16	(including some suites; all with private bathroom)	✳	Sportif
🏨	Apr–Dec	℘	18-hole golf course, tennis court, riding centre, swimming pool
✕	Light cooking methods, e.g. seafood consommé, duckling in honey and vinegar, pears in puff pastry with sabayon sauce	♫	No
		£/$	B

Château de la Commanderie

The Comtesse de Jouffray-Gonsans tells me that her family has owned la Commanderie since the 17th century, though segments of it date farther back to the 11th century. You can expect a friendly welcome at this small château in the province of Berry.

This castle belongs to Château d'Accueil and as such offers that stately private house atmosphere. The large panelled drawing room and the more intimate, adjacent library are not at all like hotel public rooms and the handsome dining room, where one may choose to dine with advance notice, is en famille, not restaurant style.

Surrounded by old trees and peaceful meadows where riding, walking and tennis may be enjoyed, the Commanderie is also well situated for touring the Route Jacques-Coeur, the Sancerre vineyards and George Sand's house.

Farges-Allichamps, 18200 St-Amand-Montrond (Cher), France. ✆ (48) 61 04 19

7	(all prettily furnished with en suite bathroom. Breakfast included)	✱	Traditional private château
		℘	Tennis and horse riding in the grounds. Arrangements may be made for hunting.
🏨	Year round		
✕	Dinner on request with advance reservation	♫	No
		£/$	B

Château de Divonne

Château de Divonne opened as a hotel in 1984 but the original castle stood here in 1095. When that was destroyed in 1589, a new one was erected only to suffer the slings and arrows of the Revolution and it was half a century later that Louis Maire-François de la Forest Divonne decided to repair his ancestral manor. It became a first class hotel during Général de Gaulle's regime when the then mayor of Divonne undertook the project of transformation.

Voltaire considered the panorama of the Mont Blanc mountains to 'be the most beautiful thing in the world' and perhaps you may agree when you view them from the windows of this château that stands above Lake Leman.

01220 Divonne-les-Bains (Ain), France. ✆ (50) 20 00 32

28	(including suites; luxuriously furnished, all with en suite bathroom)	✳	Restrained luxury
		⚐	18-hole golf course in front. Nearby fishing and sailing
🏨	Apr–Dec		
✕	Nearby La Bresse, famous for pigeons, lends a hand to the menu as do the lakes, full of trout, char, salmon and pike	♫	No
		£/$	B

Domaine de Beauvois

In the 15th century, Mace Binet was the lord of the Beauvais estate in the vicinity of Maille, the town which today is called Luynes. It was — as it is now — a perfect place for a castle, on the green banks of Lake Briffaut in the peaceful rural setting of Touraine. Look up these days and you will see the original 15th-century tower (albeit with modern windows) — other portions of the castle have been added in subsequent centuries.

During the 16th century, the castle belonged to Pierre Perronym, then Lord of Beauvais, who married Catherine de la Gaubertiere, but in the 17th century it was purchased by Charles d'Albert de Luynes to whom Louis XIII gave the title of 'Duke'. De Luynes was a personal friend of the king who frequently stayed here as a guest — his room is No. 1 in the tower, still with its original panelling and beams painted in red and gold. This is one of the most historic rooms in the hotel, so there is no TV or hairdryer as in other rooms. But you can listen to the tinkling fountain playing its merry tunes out in the courtyard and think of Louis, yet be pleased you have the modern convenience of a bathroom.

On the chimney is the coat of arms of the Earls de la Beraudiere: two silver crosses on blue and two crowned double headed eagles on red. The Beraudiere family owned Beauvois between 1789 and 1888. Although at the time of the French Revolution, those who left their estates to fight against it forfeited their lands, the Countess de la Beraudiere remained as the castle and was allowed to keep most of her property. Her husband did fight in Vendée with the royalists and only returned to Beauvais when Napoléon made it possible for emigrated nobles to come back to France. The family tombs are in the cemetery of the nearby village of Vieux-Bourg.

Domaine de Beauvois became a hotel in 1967 when it was purchased by René Traversac; its bedrooms are what give it tremendous character. No. 22 has beautiful oak panelling, for example, and No. 12 features its original fireplace and chestnut beams. The dining room is somewhat disappointing in style and you do have to step outside to reach it, but the standard of cuisine makes up for it and the wine cellar holds 40,000 bottles of prestigious wines.

Although the hotel is only 15 km (9 miles) from Tours and very close to Luynes itself, the large park which surrounds it allows tranquil hours to be spent lazing in the courtyard or by the pool. There are 140 hectares (345 acres) to explore — paths to walk, a pond for boating, trails for horse riding. Beauvois is also close to some of the Loire Valley's most famous châteaux.

37230 Luynes, Indre-et-Loire, France. ✆ (47) 55 50 11

40	(mostly double, all individually decorated, some extremely historic; all with en suite bathroom and most with TV and mini bar)	✳	Intimately medieval
		℘	Outdoor heated pool, tennis court, pond for fishing and boating, horse riding. Plenty of grounds for walking. Nearest 18-hole golf course is at Ballan Mire
🏨	Mid Mar–mid Jan		
✕	Regional specialities and nouvelle cuisine. Especially good wine cellar	♫	No
		£/$	A

Domaine de Châteauneuf

The manor house of the Châteauneuf family was built in 1680 and remained a private property until the Malets purchased it in 1929 and opened it as a hotel. Their son and his wife added their own expertise (confectionery and cake making) when they took over in 1967 and it continues to be run in family style.

Each guest room has its own decorative theme and a bathroom that features hand-painted tiles. Eighteenth-century antiques are to be admired in the entrance hall; Persian carpets warm the public rooms. The hand-painted wallpaper in the lounge dates from 1804, depicting scenes of the countryside, and the marbled fireplace here is Italian.

Châteauneuf indeed has a garden setting — petunias, geraniums and marguerites grow in unplanned profusion; shady trees encircle the swimming pool; and beyond, a large wooded park.

83860 Nans-les-Pins, la Sainte-Baume (Var), France.
℅ (94) 78 90 06

30	(including suites; all with en suite bathroom)	✳	Calm and restful
🏨	Apr–Nov	℘	Outdoor pool, 18-hole golf course, 3 tennis courts
✗	Regional cuisine, e.g. duck and pigeon Provence style	♫	No
		£/$	B

Château du Domaine Saint-Martin

Though the château you see today was built in 1936, it would seem churlish not to include it for its site is one of an ancient Templars castle. The location of the estate, overlooking Vence and the surrounding countryside to the sea, was an obvious choice for a fortified stronghold as far back as Roman times. Named for Saint-Martin, Bishop of Tours, who came here in 350, the estate was given to the crusaders in 1115 under the proviso they look after it and protect it. The Knights Templar set up a commandery therefore, whose drawbridge still stands.

In 1307 Philip the Fair eliminated the order in the hopes of laying his hands on the Templars' treasure, but the legend persists that the treasure (including a golden goat idol) remains buried somewhere. So strong is the belief that even when Mr Geneve bought the property for a hotel in 1936, the bill of sale stipulated that if any treasure was found, it was to be shared with the last owners!

The sheltered estate has welcomed numerous celebrated guests, including Truman and Adenauer, and is recommended for anyone seeking privacy. Guests who don't wish to stay in the hotel itself may opt for one of the small Provençal country houses in the grounds and still benefit from the castle services.

Décor is tasteful, not overdone: scattered Persian and

Flanders carpets and some very beautiful pieces of antique furniture. The estate provides fresh produce for the kitchen — eggs, fruit, vegetables and oil from 1000-year-old olive trees. It also has its own swimming pool and tennis court. Saint-Martin is located close to Vence and Saint-Paul, both medieval towns, but not far from the 20th-century amusements of Nice and Cannes.

06140 Route de Coursegoules, Vence (Alpes-Maritimes), France. ℘ (93) 58 02 02

25	(including villa suites with terrace; all with en suite bathroom)	✳	Luxurious
		℘	Swimming pool and tennis court in garden surrounds
🏨	Mar–mid Nov	♫	No
✕	Typical Relais French	£/$	A

Château d'Esclimont

D'Esclimont looks like everyone's idea of a beautiful French château, conveniently situated between Rambouillet and Chartres, less than an hour's drive from Paris. The present construction was built in 1543 by Étienne du Ponchet, Archbishop of Tours, and for most of its life has remained in the hands of one family. From that family have come numerous illustrious men — the Montmorencys, the Rochefoucaulds, the Lignes and the Colberts. Viscount Sosthene de la Rochefoucauld, Duke of Bisaccia, added the moats and stone bridges and enhanced the towers and façades by carved balconies and sculptures.

The Rochefoucaulds' motto was 'It's my pleasure' — no doubt, a stay here will be yours. Windows look out on to the English garden with its century-old trees, pond and river inhabited by swans and wild ducks, the moat spanned by a Renaissance bridge the main courtyard. When the weather is right, you can glide above it all in a hot-air balloon.

Esclimont has four dining rooms, one of which features leather-upholstered furniture and three of which have a view of the French garden. Bedrooms are located in the main castle, the 15th-century keep and the hunting pavilion, each lavishly furnished to a different period style. There is a room with a hideaway bed, one with a round bed, but the most unusual is the one installed in the old Duke's chapel.

Musical evenings are sometimes presented in the converted stables facing the château.

Saint-Symphorien-le-Chateau, 28700 Auneau (Eure-et-Loire), France. ✆ (37) 31 15 15

---

55 (doubles and suites; all with en suite bathroom and superb decorations)

🏨 Year round

✕ Large menu, inventive French dishes

✳ Palatial luxury

🎾 Tennis courts, swimming pool, park surrounds. Hot-air ballooning available. Nearby golf

♫ Sometimes musical evenings

£/$ A

Château du Gerfaut

Gerfaut is a hunting falcon — the best — and this small château is so named because it is situated close to the large forest where the French kings came to hunt. It is a quiet, restful place in the Loire Valley in its own wooded park, owned by the Marquis and Marquise of Chenerilles.

The Marquis tells us that part of his mother's family had the name 'Blount', one of whose members (a banker) not only clubbed together with colleagues to build the Southern Railway lines with his own station at East Grinstead, in Sussex, but in 1845, created the French 'Compagnie du Nord' — the reason, says the Marquis, that French trains run on the left!

Another ancestor, Baron Hainguerlot, lent money to Jerome Bonaparte (Napoléon's brother) and the Castle of Villandry was given to him to pay the debts of the King of Westphalia. Du Gerfaut was built in 1910 on a part of the Villandry land — the Chenerilles no longer own the château Villandry, but they still retain the forest.

This castle belongs to an association of privately owned châteaux (Châteaux d'Accueil) so don't expect a 'hotel' experience, nor the grand luxury of a Relais castle property. There are only five guest rooms and those wishing to dine here definitely need a reservation; but if you are watching the budget, this is a choice base for touring the Loire.

37190 Azay-le-Rideau (Indre et Loire), France.
✆ (47) 45 40 16

5	(rates include breakfast)	✳	Personalised
		℘	Tennis court in grounds, paths for walking or cycling
🏨	1 May–1 Aug, 1 Sep–1 Nov		
✕	Set price meals	♫	No
		£/$	C

Château
d'Isenbourg

Many centuries ago, King Dagobert chose this site for a fortress and Charlemagne, Emperor of the West, signed a charter here in the year 800. Remnants of the Middle Ages have been incorporated into the construction you see today, built in the 19th century. The gourmet restaurant, for example, has been installed in the vaulted 15th-century cellars.

Wherever you sit, the views are magnificent: towards the village of Rouffach whose red-tiled roofs are visible from the Louis XV-style panoramic restaurant's large bay windows. From the terrace across the Alsace plain and the forest of the Vosges, to the large feudal courtyard immediately in front of the hotel with its round ornamental lake, to the vineyards of Alsace, for this site between Strasbourg and Thann is along the famous Route des Vins.

D'Isenbourg has retained its medieval character with its antiques and restored sculpted ceilings.

68250 Rouffach (Haut-Rhin), France. ⌀ **(89) 49 63 53**

40	(including suites; all individually styled with en suite bathroom)	✳	Quietly gracious
		℘	Heated pool, tennis court in park
🏨	Apr–Dec	♬	No
✕	Regional dishes	£/$	B

Château de Locguénolé

Anyone who thinks that the titled French nobility don't work, should definitely overnight at the Château de Locguénolé. It has been the family seat of the de la Sablieres since 1200, but Countess Alyette de la Sabliere (patrician as she is) was forced to turn her castle into a hotel to make ends meet, and had to take herself off to business school to ensure the project worked. It is quite obvious she has made a remarkable achievement with Michelin rosettes for cuisine and praise from guests who are happy enough to pay high prices for haute grandeur.

As the Celtic prefix of the château's name suggests, this stately home is situated on the banks of the River Blavet quite close to the Breton resorts of Port-Louis, Carnac and Quiberon. Like others of its ilk, it took major restoration work after the Revolution so that much of the present building was constructed around 1800. There was more work to be done after the Liberation when the de la Sablieres returned to Hennebont, for German admirals had used the property as their headquarters and what they didn't manage to destroy, American bombs did.

However, there is no lack of luxury now. Family portraits adorn the walls along with Flemish tapestries. Much of the furniture is over 100 years old and there are five reception rooms (including one for music) where guests tend to gather before and after dinner. Some people may find the atmosphere a little cool and formal but others will simply feel they are staying in a grand and private house.

The greatest pride at Locguénolé is the food, presented beautifully and highly recommended to the true gourmet. The peaceful setting in a park planted with age-old trees and crossed by bridle paths is another plus factor. Locguénolé has its own swimming pool and tennis court and is located 5 km (3 miles) from Hennebont, 15 km (9 miles) from Lorient airport.

Route de Port-Louis, 56700 Hennebont (Morbihan), France. ∅ (97) 76 29 04

36	(32 doubles, 4 suites; all with en suite bathroom, some with TV)	✳	Genteel
		℘	Outdoor pool, tennis court in the grounds. Fishing on the River Blavet and hunting may be arranged. Horse riding and sailing nearby. Beaches 9 km (5½ miles). The nearest 18-hole golf course is 20 km (12½ miles)
🏛	Mar–Nov		
✕	Imaginative and gastronomic. Award winning		
		♫	No
		£/$	B

Château de Mercuès

Château de Mercuès has seen religious wars and revolution, fire and destruction. It has been a temple, fortress and a residence — the property of the noble clergy of Cahors for almost twelve centuries, now lovingly restored. Where the 'Orangerie' suites are now situated was the main building of the 1212 fortress. In the 14th century, as the castle increased in size, the village of Mercuès was established at the foot of the hill. By the 15th century, then almost in ruins, an even grander château was erected. Terraces and gardens were added in the 17th century while 20th-century refinements included lifts and a swimming pool.

An aristocrat among castle hotels, this one has handsome décor, wooded grounds and excellent views. Cahors is 8 km (5 miles) away and Toulouse airport, 90 km (56 miles).

46090 Cahors (Lot), France. ∅ (65) 20 00 01

23	(doubles and suites; all with en suite bathroom and TV)	✳	Noble, restful
		℘	Swimming pool, 2 tennis courts, walks in the wooded grounds. Arrangements may be made for hunting and fishing
🏠	Apr–Oct		
✗	Typically Relais French, e.g. magret de canard, chocolate marquise		
		♫	No
		£/$	B

Château du Molay

This beautiful Normandy country mansion was built in 1758 by Jacques le Couteulx, King Louis XV's equerry. It was his first grand residence, located close to Rouen, his birthplace and is now, as it was then, surrounded by wooded grounds. The architectural style visible today, however, is due to the work, 75 years later, of Edouard, Count of Chabrol-Crousol, member of the House of Peers during Napoléon III's reign and an avid collector of books and art.

At the end of the 19th century the château was the property of the Viellard family — the setting for 50 years' worth of festive occasions until the Second World War when the Germans used it as a launching ground for the V2s.

14330 le Molay-Littry (Normandie), France.
✆ (31) 22 90 82

38	(all with private bathroom)	✳	Restful
		℘	Large heated pool with
🏠	Mar–Nov		solarium, relaxation room
✕	Light food prepared		with spa, sauna, uv
	Normandy style		suntanning equipment,
			massages. Tennis court
		♫	No
		£/$	C

Château de Monviel

The first building on this site was in the 9th century — still existent wells date from this era. In the 13th century a fortress was erected. Remnants of the Three Hundred Year War period also remain: the bread ovens, the underground passage that led to the chapel of Monviel and the grotto carved from the rock. From 1577 to almost the 19th century, the castle belonged to the Vassals, who transformed it into a seigniorial manor. It became a hotel in 1982.

Château de Monviel has a monumental entrance hall with stone steps leading to bedroom accommodation on the first floor. Set amid flowers and trees in the calm country of the Lot and Garonne, it is not a grandiose place to stay, but it is a private one. You'll find a small private pool on the terrace and enjoy home cooking and regional wines in the dining room. Bergerac airport is 35 km (22 miles) away.

Monviel, 47290 Cancon (Lot-et-Garonne), France.
∅ (53) 01 71 64

10	(including 1 suite; all with en suite bathroom)	✳	Simple comforts
🏨	Apr–mid Nov	℘	Outdoor pool. Nearby tennis, riding, fishing and golf
✗	Fresh local produce, e.g. home-made foies gras and confits		
		♫	No
		£/$	C

Château de Nieuil

No noise at this superb Renaissance-style château, formerly one of François I's hunting lodges, for it is surrounded by 32 hectares (80 acres) of wooded park which itself is part of a much larger estate. A moat encircles the castle, a building which is flanked by two round towers with pointed roofs and looks on to a formal French garden. François I ceded the Nieuil land to the Grunn family in whose hand it stayed until the reign of Louis XV. Around 1750, through marriage, it became the property of the Perry family. It was one of the first châteaux to become a hotel — opening in 1937 under the supervision of the current proprietor's grandfather.

The interior is very much of the François I period: a commanding marble staircase in the entrance hall, Aubusson tapestries and magnificent carpets, oil paintings, polished wood, antique furniture including an enormous table made from one solid piece of elm.

Imprinted as it is with several generations of French nobility, Château de Nieuil is surprisingly unstuffy and unpretentious. Thanks to the owner, Michel Bodinaud, this hotel manages to be both sophisticated, yet friendly. Napery is starched, room drapes are long, crystal chandeliers gleam, but everywhere is softened by flowers — on plates as well as tables.

Madame Bodinaud commands the kitchen and has won coveted awards for her efforts, be they traditional French or modern mixtures, served in the grand formal dining room or al fresco buffet by the pool. Her husband, an art buff as well as hotelier, uses the former stables to exhibit and sell modern works of art.

16270 Nieuil (Charente), France. ✆ (45) 71 36 38

15	(including suites; all with private bathroom and views of the lawn or French flower garden)	✳	Personalised stately
		℘	Swimming pool, tennis court, fishing
🏨	Late Apr–mid Nov	♬	No
✕	Local dishes and modern ones, using regional produce and vegetables from the château garden	£/$	C

Pavillon Henri IV

Who can resist a stay in a royal birthplace (Louis XIV entered the world here), or indeed who can resist sitting where Alexander Dumas wrote *The Three Musketeers*?

In the 16th century, two castles existed in St-Germain-en-Laye of which the Pavillon is the remains of the newer. It was Henri II and Catherine de Medici who decided to build a small mansion for their leisure, a bath house down on the River Seine, and between the two, gardens and terraces converted from vineyards. But it was Henri IV who turned the modest residence into an imposing Italiante palace and gave the terraces their richness. The Doric Terrace, under which were beautiful caves, still exists today but the marble panelled Tuscan Terrace has disappeared. Underneath the latter there were many beautiful caves, decorated with precious stones and rocks from around the world and containing unusual curiosities.

Thanks to Henry IV, this 'new' castle became the favourite royal residence, almost exclusively lived in by Louis XIII in whose apartment the young dauphin, Louis XIV, was born, to be christened in the chapel, now part of the hotel. He spent most of his youth in the castle and his early married years. When the castle was given to the dethroned Stuarts (as Louis XIV made Versailles his official residence), it was the beginning of decay for the new castle, its fabulous caves left to ruin because they were too costly to maintain.

In 1777, Louis XIV gave the castle to his brother, the Count of Artois, with money meant for its restoration. But the latter prince considered the one-floor palace too small and laid out plans for a much more ostentatious establishment.

Destroy it though he did, the northern part of that 'new' castle — the Chapel of the King — is where you'll stay today. In 1820, it was referred to (according to the land registry office) as 'property of the Crown'. At the time no one wanted the neglected building, until it was rented by Mr Collinet, famous for his invention of soufflé potatoes and Bernaise sauce — who turned the place into a hotel, one of whose favoured customers was Alexander Dumas.

Today the Pavillon warrants its four star de luxe rating with luxurious guest rooms (well equipped), elegant drawing rooms and a dining room that all retain regal style. You will find superb Asian carpets, Italian marbles and French antiques; you will find panoramic views of the Seine and mouthwatering cuisine.

Pavillon Henri IV is located within about a half hour's drive from Paris in what has become a stylish suburb.

St-Germain-en-Laye, 78100 (Yvelines), France.
✆ (1) 34 51 62 62

45	(including suites; all with en suite bathroom)	✳	Intimately regal
🏨	Year round	℘	Guests at the Pavillon have sports privileges at a nearby
✗	Such specialities as red mullet terrine, stuffed pigeon and, of course, bœuf Bernaise		club with indoor and outdoor tennis, squash courts, putting green and pool. The adjacent park has paths for jogging and cycling
		♫	Piano music
		£/$	A

Le Prieure

Le Prieure has an outstanding hilltop position on the left bank of the Loire in the middle of some of France's most famous wine country. Some of the arched windows from the 12th-century building which stood here still exist on the northern façade, though much of the château dates from the 16th century. For several centuries it was a Benedictine monastery, hence its name. After the order was disbanded, it passed through several owners until Comte de Castellane purchased it in the 20th century and started restoration. Le Prieure became a hotel in 1955.

A spiral stone staircase leads down from the entrance to the reception, a small formal bar, large cocktail lounge, a sun terrace with magnificent views and a handsomely appointed dining room. Some of the guest rooms are in the main part of the château; others are reached at terrace level.

The charming village of Tuffeaux is only 6 km (4 miles) from Saumur, guarded by its own castle.

Chenehutte-les-Tuffeaux, 49350 Gennes (Maine-et-Loire), France. ✆ (41) 67 90 14

40	(mostly twin, some in the main house, some bungalows in the grounds; all with en suite bathroom, TV and hairdryer)	✳	Elegant
		℘	Heated pool, tennis, mini golf, pétanque. Nearby fishing
🏠	Mar–Dec	♫	No
✗	Fancy French nouvelle	£/$	A

Château de Prunoy

An enchantingly peaceful setting and the chance to stay in a Regency château that is a listed building — that is what Prunoy offers, in a region well known for its scenery and good food.

In 1510 Guillaume de Crevecoeur chose this site to build a lovely manor. What remains from the 16th century today is the Library Tower, a round tower at the end of the left wing, but most of the château dates from the 18th century when typical period architecture called for 'through rooms', when you can look through the front windows to the grounds at the back. The four reception rooms in the central part of Prunoy show this aspect and date from the time François Christophe de Lalive made his alterations in 1721, as do the square-crowned small towers on the sides of the building. In 1779, Ange-Laurent Lalive de Jully had the grounds landscaped and the fish ponds (designed by the school of Lenotre) installed, at the far end of the grounds. They are annually maintained by the addition of carp and perch and, every 20 or so years, emptied and the fish sold.

Abandoned during the Revolution, by 1838 Prunoy had become the possession of a nephew of the Lalive line — Raymond Aymery, Duke of Montesquieu-Fezensac and one of Napoléon's ex-generals. The same year he was named as French ambassador to Spain. When his daughter Henriette

Oriane inherited the château in 1867, she and her husband, Comte de Goyon, brought new life and gaiety to the place which stayed the family residence until the beginning of this century when it was sold to the Rameras. Since Ramera was an active member of the Neo-Pagan (Bloomsbury) group and welcomed other members, it is sure conversation wasn't lacking at that time!

Today's proprietor ensures guests are comfortable in spacious, floral decorated rooms and in the restaurant where the best of the region's produce is used. Each of the guest rooms is named and the one available suite boasts its own sauna. Prunoy is located 23 km (14 miles) from Joigny, 45 km (28 miles) from Auxerre.

89120 Charny (Yonne), France. ✆ (86) 63 66 91

13	(12 doubles or twins, 1 suite with its own sauna, each individually styled; all with en suite bathroom)	✳	Family style, comfortably friendly
		℘	Tennis, hunting and fishing
⌂	Late Mar–early Jan	♪	discothèque
✗	Home cooking, fixed price menus	£/$	C

Château de Puy Robert

This charming small castle dates from the Napoléon III era, and stands on a knoll dominating the Vézère Valley, facing the caves of Lascaux. It was transformed into a four star hotel in 1986.

In the main house there are drawing rooms, a bar and two restaurants, graced with white linen and a fabric-ed ceiling. The majority of the bedrooms are in a superbly converted outbuilding, all furnished with genuine or reproduction antique furniture and flowery papers and curtains. Balconied or terraced, they look on to the gardens and park.

Set in the heart of Périgord, Château de Puy Robert is 3 km (2 miles). From Montignac whose caves and prehistoric paintings are famous. From here it is equally easy to visit Sarlat and les Ezies.

24290 Montignac en Périgord (Dordogne), France.
✆ (53) 51 92 13

38 (including suites; all with private bathroom)	✳	Romantic
🏠 Jun–Oct	℘	Outdoor pool. Tennis (under construction at time of writing). Horse riding nearby
✕ Modern dishes and regional specialities		
	♫	No
	£/$	B

Château du Riau

Perhaps surprisingly, Château du Riau has survived not only the test of time, but civil wars and revolution, too, so its 15th-, 16th- and 17th-century sections are all intact. It is a listed historic monument, open to the public, but it has always been — and is — a family home, close to the birthplace of the Bourbon royal family.

It was a goldsmith from nearby Moulins by the name of Charles Popillon who acquired a small 14th-century château, on whose foundations he built Riau in 1480. You will see the 15th-century entrance tower with its mullion windows, and under the château's slate roof is a 15th-century staircase and rooms furnished in 18th-century fashion. The outbuildings and pigeon house, all within the moat, date from the 16th and 17th centuries, but outside is one of the most interesting — the 'dime' barn, half-timbered and built of multi-coloured bricks by Nicolas Roger who signed his work as carpenter in 1584.

Charles Popillon was to become treasurer and eventually president of the Chambre des Comptes in Moulins, thanks to the Bourbon duchesses, particularly Louis XI's daughter, Anne de Beaujeu. The castle has only know four resident families. After the Popillons, the influential Nivernais family, the de Charrys, occupied du Riau from 1700 to 1803. During this time, Arthur Young was one of the Admiral de

Charry's English guests who described his stay with such admiration in 1789. Then came the Boigues family from Decize and finally in 1826 Pierre Le Roy de Chavigny, Prefect of the Allier, purchased the property in 1826 and it is his descendants, the Duryes, who run the estate today.

Guest accommodation is limited but irresistible and all overnight guests are welcomed with a kir (white wine and cassis). It's an atmospheric spot for an overnight stop in the centre of Bourbon country.

03460 Villeneuve-sur-Allier (Allier), France.
☎ (70) 43 30 74

3	(1 double, 1 twin, 1 suite for 4 people, all with bathroom. Rates include breakfast)	✳	Historic
		℘	No, but swimming, tennis, riding and golfing facilities not far away
🏰	Year round	♫	No
✗	Exceptional table d'hôte evening meal by request	£/$	C

Château de Rochegude

There was a fortress of Rochegude in Roman times, mentioned in archives three centuries after the birth of Christ. When excavations were made of the castle's cellars in 1820, a magnificent and rare Roman-era statue of Bacchus was discovered tucked into a wall niche, no doubt hidden from attackers in the 16th century (the sculpture now adorns the museum in St-Germain-en-Laye).

Much of the château today was constructed in the 12th century when Guillaume de Mondragon and Hughes de Caderousse were the lords. It is known that the 14th-century popes chose the castle to be their court of justice and that room of justice still exists. After a destructive attack by the Baron des Adrets in the 16th century, the castle declined until the end of Louis XIV's reign when reconstruction made the building less of a fort and more of a residence. A monumental staircase was built and, later, the craftsmen who worked on Marie Antoinette's 'Petit Trianon' created the decorative plaster work that abounds in the hotel now.

Marble and alabaster statuary graces both the interior and the grounds. You will find red velvet-covered walls, carved wooden pillars and chests, marvellous ceilings. In other words, a host of antiques and some very grand rooms. Lit up at night, Rochegude presents a truly magnificent sight.

Whether you eat in the elegant dining room or breakfast

on the terrace in the open air, there are treats in store like the home-grown plums and the castle's own wine. Grounds are spacious with a tennis court and oversized pool while excursion possibilities include Orange, 14 km (9 miles) away.

26790 Rochegude (Drôme), France. ✆ (75) 04 81 88

29	(mostly double, some suites; all with en suite bathroom, most very grand)	✳	Fine living
		℘	Swimming pool, tennis
		♫	No
🏨	Mar–Dec, but also from mid-Tues to mid-Wed every week	£/$	B
✕	Traditional French		

Château de Roumegouse

The 14th century saw the merge of the Houses of Castlenau and Gramat and Roumegouse became a key defence for Hughes II of Castelnau, one of the most powerful lords of Aquitaine. Like many another French fortified castle, this one was destroyed and rebuilt several times over the centuries of warring and was in ruins when the feudal system came to an end.

What you find today is a reconstruction started by Jean Pisie in 1893 and finished in 1895.

The family atmosphere is complemented by thoughtful décor — flowers everywhere, pastels, heart-shaped-backed chairs in the breakfast room. Situated in 5 hectares (12 acres) of parkland on a hilltop facing the 'Causse' of Rocamadour, this hushed little castle hotel is 65 km (40 miles) from medieval Sarlat and 60 km (37 miles) from Cahors.

Rignac 46500 Gramat (Lot), France. ✆ **(65) 33 63 81**

16	(including suites; all with en suite bathroom, colour TV and mini bar)	✳	Family charm
		℘	No, but nearby swimming and tennis
🏛	Apr–Oct	♫	No
✕	Sauces a speciality	£/$	B

Château de la Salle

It has stored grain, been a prison and was a headquarters base for the Germans during the Second World War, but this château's story really starts in the 11th century with the Cambernon family whose 16th-century descendant, Marguerite de Cambernon, married an Olivier Martel in 1532. Parts of the 16th-century structure remain today, rediscovered during a later century restoration. Marguerite's grand-daughter married a Louis Caillebot who became Marquis de la Salle in 1673 and the de la Salle family lived at Montpinchon until 1789.

Around 1796, the château housed Spanish prisoners captured by Napoléon's army. After a fire destroyed the second floor, it was used as a farm building for some 150 years until the Lemesle-Leclerc family took it over in 1900. Nowadays, the lady of the house, Cecile Lemesle (who doesn't speak English) presides over this intimate and restful small château — especially the vaulted dining room with its large fireplace, once the old kitchen. There are only 11 tables, all neatly laid with lacy tablecloths and candles, graced by tall-backed tapestried chairs.

You certainly feel as if you're staying in an old castle at Château de la Salle, for there are massive pieces of furniture including an original 16th-century four poster bed which, because it is original, is less wide than the normal double beds we're used to. The hotel is also rather dark, especially the older section (which has more atmosphere). Lighter rooms, but with less character, are Nos. 7–10.

It is a very peaceful place, located between Mont Saint-Michel and the Allied landing beaches — southwest of Coutances in the valley of the Soulle.

50210 Montpinchon (Manche), France. ✆ (33) 46 95 19

10	(including four poster; all with en suite bathroom and colour TV)	✳	Genuine castle character, but too gloomy for some
🏨	Mar–Oct	℘	None on site. The nearest swimming pool is at Coutances, the nearest golf at Granville (30 km, 18½ miles)
✗	Small quantities of superb French nouvelle food, e.g. crab salad with grapefruit as a starter, followed by brill in a butter wine sauce that looks as if it's made with cream		
		♫	No
		£/$	C

Château de Teildras

They sing about Anjou, write poems about this enchanting part of France. The Château de Teildras fits into this picture superbly for it is the small ancestral home of the du Breil family who have owned it since the 16th century. Today, it is still the Count Bernard du Breil who invites you to enjoy the undisturbed tranquillity of his white-walled, grey-roofed hostelry. Some years ago, he decided the best way to preserve his estate was to turn it into a hotel and he has succeeded in creating a commercially viable establishment that is entrancing.

You may well agree that the atmosphere is soothing and restful and the furnishings tasteful. Tapestries and paintings decorate the walls of the dining room and other public areas; plants and flowers bedeck the terraces and garden. The lighting is subdued, the ceilings beamed, and antiques and old books are liberally scattered.

Cheffes-sur-Sarthe, 49125 Tierce, (Maine-et-Loire), France. ✆ (41) 42 61 08

11	(all double with en suite bathroom, TV)	✳	Discreet atmosphere
🏨	Apr–Nov	♞	Walks in the park, river fishing, tennis
✕	Typical of a Relais hotel— plenty of good Anjou wines	♫	No
		£/$	B

Château de Thaumiers

A place where Viscount and Viscountess de Bonneval offer to share their family life in a French château for a few days. It is elegant and historic, for the first towers were built in the 15th century. This was the time when Bourges was the capital of France and many castles were erected for defence purposes. The work of Jean de la Forest was completed by his son, resulting in a square fortress with four corner towers, surrounded by moats and a drawbridge.

A century later, Madeleine de l'Auberpine was lady of the manor and encouraged the arts, but it was Henriette de Doulle, the 18th-century owner, who decided the fortress seemed too severe and made several alterations to 'soften' its appearance, including large French windows opening on to the park.

Thaumiers, 18210 Charenton-du-Cher (Cher), France.
℘ (48) 61 81 62

12	(including suites and a self-catering wing; all with bathroom)	✳	Friendly and quiet
🏰	Mar–Nov	℘	Tennis, practice golf. Pool 10 km (6 miles) away, riding, 20 km (12 miles)
✕	Really B & B. Dinner on request only	♫	No
		£/$	B

Château de Trigance

It certainly looks like a genuine castle and it certainly dominates the village of Trigance whose stone houses make a rampart. Originally, the fortress on this rocky spur was dedicated to meditation, and was created by the monks of the St. Victor Abbey in the ninth century. Then it became the possession of the Counts of Provence.

Destroyed in the Revolution, the château for long served as a quarry for the village inhabitants — until 1961, when the Hartmanns fell in love with the ruins and began restoration, a project that was continued ten years later by another couple, Mr and Mrs Thomas.

Now that it offers modern day comforts within its medieval walls, Château de Trigance is easy to adore, though you can only reach it via a steep rocky path and stone stairway. Naturally, from the top, there are splendid views of the rocky hills around it, especially from the large terrace.

83840 Trigance (Var), France. ✆ (94) 76 91 18

8	(double, 1 suite, some canopied beds; all with en suite bathroom, some with TV)	✳	Restful, medieval
		✌	No
		♪	No
		£/$	B
🏨	Apr–Oct		
✕	Regional specialities		

Château de la Vallée Bleue

This is more of a grand house than a castle, built in 1840 by Doctor Pestel who moved here from Paris to be closer to his patient, George Sand (whose former home, Nohant, is not far away). Although only a two star hotel it is a find for those on a budget seeking somewhere peaceful. Each of its 15 guest rooms is named for a composer and you can be prepared for a good table since the owner is the chef!

Located just outside the small village of Saint-Chartier, Château de la Vallée Bleue has its own 4-hectare (10-acre) park and is 8 km (5 miles) from la Chatre.

Saint-Chartier, 36400 la Chatre (Berry), France.
☏ (54) 31 01 91

15	(12 rooms are in the main building; all with bath or shower, most with WC)	✳	Simple and calm
		℘	No
▥	Easter–mid Jan	♫	No
✗	Regional wines and down-to-earth French cooking	£/$	C

Château de la Verrerie

Anglo-French hospitality at its best is offered in this beautiful 15th-century castle by the Count and Countess of Vogue. Its setting, in front of a lake and surrounded by forest, combined with private country home cachet, makes this a splendid base from which to explore the Route Jacques-Coeur.

The castle was built by Beraud Stuart. Reminders of the Scottish royals are evident in the chapel's frescoes and the loggia erected in 1525 by Robert Stuart of Lennox when he returned from the Italian wars. King Charles II's mistress, the Duchess of Portsmouth, lived here between 1672 and 1734 and her descendants, the dukes of Richmond, sold the estate to Marquis de Vogue in 1842 — whose grandson is the present owner.

Oizon, 18700 Aubigny-sur-Nère) (Cher), France.
✆ (48) 58 06 91

7	(doubles, individually decorated; all with private bathroom)	✳ Cheerful nobility
		℘ In the park, private tennis court, swimming, riding and forest walks
🏨	Mar–Oct	
✕	Regional specialities and wine	♫ No
		£/$ B

Le Vieux Castillon

Unique and off the beaten track, this château comprises several old manor houses that have been cleverly converted into one complex, set on a rocky promontory 3 km (2 miles) from the Pont du Gard. So peaceful is the setting today, you could scarcely believe it was the scene of religious blood baths in the past. From the watchpath leading to the fortified church the view now is pleasurable — over vineyards, olive and fig trees. Here, a small garden with a profusion of flowers, there a little bridge, and over there a terrace by the side of a pool.

The Fumoir dining room and bar, under an arched stone ceiling and with a feature stone fireplace, opens on to the terrace, overlooking the ramparts and surrounding country-side. Guest rooms are individually furnished in styles that range from rustic to elegant.

Castillon du Gard, 30210 Remoulins (Gard), France.
℘ **(66) 37 00 77**

35	(mostly double, individually decorated; all with en suite bathroom)	✳	Peaceful, relaxing
		♀	Outdoor pool, tennis court. Nearby fishing
▥	Apr–Dec	♪	No
✕	Provençal cuisine based on seasonal produce	£/$	B

Hôtel du Vieux Château

Deep in the heart of Normandy, this hotel is an integral part of an ancient castle that dates back to 912 when Rollon Ansleck of Bastembourg formed the family tree of the Bertrands, lords of Bricquebec. One of these lords, Le Tors, was indeed an aide to William on his conquest of England and another, Robert Bertrand VII, conquered Guernsey in 1339.

Through marriage the castle became the property of the Paynel family, but when the English captured it in 1418, the estate passed to Guillaume de la Polle, Count of Suffolk, who was later made a prisoner by Joan of Arc. In 1450 it was returned to the Paynels and, again through marriage, passed to the Longuevilles, the Matignons and finally the Montmorencys.

Hotel apart, it is worth looking around the castle complex. In the clock tower you'll find a regional museum and from the top, the best view of the whole area. The Charter Room's vaulted cellar dates from the 15th century and there is plenty more to see in the crypt, the keep and the Thorn Tower. The hotel itself is actually the oldest part of the castle, probably originally one huge room which opened on to the courtyard through four 12th-century Gothic arches.

The upper part of this Knights Hall is still visible in the hotel attic. But you can rest assured that guest rooms provide modern comforts and you won't have to eat with your hands.

4 cours du Château, 50260 Bricquebec (Normandie), France. ⌀ **(33) 52 24 49**

22	(all with private bathroom)	✳	Very much the Norman castle
🏨	Feb–Nov	℘	No, but nearby tennis and horse riding
✕	Traditional French	♫	No
		£/$	C

Château de la Vigne

Towered and parapeted la Vigne was built in the 15th century by the lords of Scorailles on the site of an even earlier castle. Generations of the same family lived here until 1745 when it became part of the marriage dowry of Anne-Charlotte to Bertrand d'Humieres, and it was he who styled it as it is today. The castle survived the Revolution without damage, becoming the property of the de la Tour d'Auvergne family through further marriage.

Antique lovers will find much to admire here from the wood-panelled reception rooms to the family portraits displayed on the walls and the exceptional furniture. Aubusson tapestries in the grand salon depict mythological scenes; impressive fireplaces and high ceilings are other features. Murals, a secret passage, canopied beds and fancy faience are among the delights of the guest rooms. The former chapel with its painted, vaulted ceiling and the wonderfully decorated justice room have to be seen to be believed.

Ally, 15700 Pleaux (Cantal), France ✆ (71) 69 00 20

4	(2 doubles, 2 suites for 4 people. Rates include breakfast)	✳	Very historic
		℘	4 tennis courts in the park. Nearby riding
▥	Jul and Aug	♫	No
✗	Dinner not available	£/$	C

GERMANY

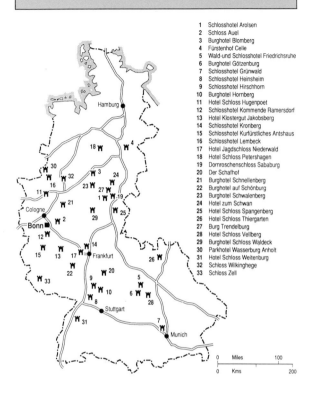

1 Schlosshotel Arolsen
2 Schloss Auel
3 Burghotel Blomberg
4 Fürstenhof Celle
5 Wald-und Schlosshotel Friedrichsruhe
6 Burghotel Götzenburg
7 Schlosshotel Grünwald
8 Schlosshotel Heinsheim
9 Schlosshotel Hirschhorn
10 Burghotel Hornberg
11 Hotel Schloss Hugenpoet
12 Schlosshotel Kommende Ramersdorf
13 Hotel Klostergut Jakobsberg
14 Schlosshotel Kronberg
15 Schlosshotel Kurfürstliches Antshaus
16 Schlosshotel Lembeck
17 Hotel Jagdschloss Niederwald
18 Hotel Schloss Petershagen
19 Dornroschenschloss Sababurg
20 Der Schafhof
21 Burghotel Schnellenberg
22 Burghotel auf Schönburg
23 Burghotel Schwalenberg
24 Hotel zum Schwan
25 Hotel Schloss Spangenberg
26 Hotel Schloss Thiergarten
27 Burg Trendelburg
28 Hotel Schloss Vellberg
29 Burghotel Schloss Waldeck
30 Parkhotel Wasserburg Anholt
31 Hotel Schloss Weitenburg
32 Schloss Wilkinghege
33 Schloss Zell

Germany's castles are legendary and ubiquitous. After the last world war, many were converted into hotels as the only way of keeping them in existence. Just over 25 years ago, the Gast im Schloss consortium was formed to assist such hotels to become recognised.

Their history is especially important so a number of the Gast im Schloss hotels are included here. As hotels, they are generally not very large, are often family run and offer excellent value for money for anyone who enjoys the idea of being a guest in a castle. They are more likely to be gemütlich (cosy, atmospheric) than luxurious and are usually located well away from city centres.

A noticeable feature of German castle hotels are their wedding chapels in the grounds which are frequently used for that very purpose. There is almost always at least one bridal room or honeymoon suite, usually with the best view and setting — in a tower perhaps — often with a four poster bed. Several of the hotels also specialise in 'Knights' Feasts' or similar, in keeping with their historic backgrounds.

Schlosshotel Arolsen

The palace was built in the 18th century by Franz-Friedrich Rothweil for Prince Carl's widow. After her death, Emma, Princess of Anhalt-Bernburg, had the building changed, replacing the rococo furnishings with then fashionable stucco decoration. You will see a beautiful stuccoed ceiling when you climb the main staircase.

Arolsen's major asset is that it is directly connected to a medical spa centre and the hotel features two, three or four week programmes that include acupuncture, beauty treatments, exercise routines and wholemeal diets, as well as a wholemeal cooking and baking course. Whether or not guests take the course they can opt for a wholemeal menu in the dining room, and at breakfast time, items like homemade marmalades, raw cereals and full grain rolls are on the buffet along with more 'normal' foods. Indeed, the hotel's own small mill grinds flour freshly and herbs and vegetables come from the palace garden.

Those not dieting can indulge in more fattening fare (a Knights' Feast perhaps) or refreshments in the lounge that was the former barrel vaults.

3548 Arolsen, Grosse Allee 1, Germany. ✆ (05691) 3091

58	(mostly double, including suites)	✳	Palatial spa
		℘	Indoor and outdoor

🏨 Year round

✕ Wholemeal items include cabbage leaves stuffed with mushrooms, rye and millet noodles with spinach

swimming pools, sauna, tennis, shooting range, full medical centre. Riding and jogging paths in vicinity. Swimming possible in the Twiste lake — angling, sailing and surfing on the Twiste reservoir.

♫ Knights' Banquets; speciality weekends

£/$ C

Schloss Auel

If you have a sense of humour and like to talk flying, you'll find Schloss Auel — and its congenial baron host — exceptionally jolly. Frhr. von la Valette St George can trace his family tree back to the oldest French nobility, descendants of the Dukes of Rouergue. His most famous ancestor was, of course, Jean de la Valette, who became Grand-Master of the Order of St John of Jerusalem and later of the Maltese Order, successfully defending the island of Malta against the Turks in 1565.

More direct lineage stems from the young French officer, Jean Paul de la Valette, who arrived in Cologne in the 18th century and whose grandson, Philippe, acquired this castle through marriage. Today's baron will tell you plenty of anecdotes about his family and their eccentric ways but since he is a passionate pilot, he holds lengthy conversations about aviation besides, especially during his annual helicopter fly-in. He heartily explains his castle hotel as having 'romance, rotation, relaxation — one more R than Rolls-Royce'.

The building itself acquired its three-winged appearance under Philippe de la Valette St George's ownership, but as a castle, Auel existed in 1391 and later became the family seat of the von Meuchens and the von Proff zu Mendens. The la Valette St George family acquired German nationality at the end of the last century through the present baron's great-grandfather, Adolf, a great friend of Kaiser Wilhelm II.

Auel has never wanted for famous guests. Before it was welcoming the general public in 1951, it was welcoming crowned heads of State. Napoléon stayed here in 1811 — and you can sleep in his very room, No. 22 (though the bed has been extended for we taller people). The Kaiser was obviously a frequent guest (his suite may also be used). The guest book will also shown that Shirley Temple, Princess Soraya and Henry Ford II have been among others to have slept here.

The most impressive room is the entrance hall with its Renaissance furniture and heavy chests, and a fine oak staircase leading to the bedrooms. Not that the rest of the hotel is without Gobelins, paintings and crystal chandeliers. the castle chapel (many Germany castle hotels have these which may be used for wedding ceremonies) is especially beautiful with a rococo altar and 16th- and 17th-century artwork.

In a green spot between Bonn and Cologne (both of which cities are well worth visiting), Schloss Auel does offer guests a number of facilities of its own, from an indoor swimming pool to a rifle range. Just watch out for the castle's pet geese!

5204 Lohmar 21 (Wahlscheid), Germany.
✆ **(02206) 2041**

23	(mostly double, four poster Napoléon room; all with en suite bathroom and TV)	✳	Jolly
🏨	Year round	℘	Indoor swimming pool with sauna, tennis court
✗	Specialities include game in pastry, duck, loin of venison, and fresh trout from nearby rivers		adjacent to hotel. Bowling alley, air rifle range and riding stables. Also heliport
		♪	No
		£/$	C

Burghotel Blomberg

For 300 years, Blomberg Castle was the favourite residence of Lippe nobility with its Renaissance façade and thick fortified walls. It is thought the earliest structure was founded in the 13th century by Lord Bernhard III zur Lippe. The castle was willed to the Lippe-Brake line of the family and eventually to the House of Schaumburg-Lippe. Bought by the City in 1962, it became a hotel in 1971.

Burghotel Blomberg is somewhat more commercialised than many other German castle hotels: weddings often take place here with full fanfare and coach, and medieval banquets are staged in the summer, as are torch-lit evening dances and concerts. Feasts in the King Arthur mode are followed by old court games and archery, and entertainment may be anything from court jester to magician or fire-eater.

4933 Blomberg, Germany ✆ (05235) 2071

50	(mostly double)	✳	A sense of activity
⌂	Year round	℘	Indoor swimming pool and sauna; outdoor pool in the forest. Tennis in town
✕	Recommended is 'Lippische Pickert' with green pepper and local juniper-smoked trout	♫	Medieval feasts and other summertime festivities
		£/$	C

Fürstenhof Celle

This baroque palace is noted for outstanding service and praiseworthy cuisine. It was built by master architect Francesco Maria Cappelini Stechinelli around 1670 and, after the duchy of Celle became extinct at the beginning of the 18th century, was the residence of Carl Friedrich Count of Hardenberg until 1817 when Friedrich August von der Osten bought the estate. In 1969, Christian Count of Hardenberg bought the palace in memory of his ancestor and converted it into a gracious hotel.

The aristocratic touch is evident the moment you enter the foyer with its mirror-coffered ceiling and historic wall panelling from Schwuper Castle. A look around will show you the elegant Blue Salon on the first floor with its stuccoed ceiling and fine chandelier. In the von Osten room the walls are covered with painted canvas and in another room there is hand-painted wallpaper from the Empire period.

Guest rooms are modern but the vaulted cellar used as a bar is 300 years old. The old method of catching ducks was by using a 'fang' — an oblong pond with funnel-shaped pipes. Wild ducks, having been attracted by decoys, were frightened by a sudden noise and caught by nets as they hastily flew to the light exit of the canal-catch. The new method is somewhat different, but duck is still the speciality of the gourmet Endtenfang Restaurant (roast duck was the favourite of the dukes of Braunschweig-Luneburg). Duck paintings decorate the walls and, if requested, the duck-press (used to squeeze juice from the bones) is worked at the table. The alternative Kutscherstuben restaurant is a more rustic retreat.

The hotel has its own swimming pool, sauna and solarium and a beer pub with bowling alley. Celle is located a 35-minute journey from Hannover-Langenhagen airport.

3100 Celle, Hannoversche Strasse 55/56, Germany.
✆ (05141) 2010

75	(including suites; all with en suite bathroom)	✳	Sophisticated
⌕	Year round	℘	Swimming pool with sauna and solarium, bowling alley. Nearest golf course at Burgdof, 12 km (7½ miles) away. Outdoor pool, riding, angling, tennis at Celle
✕	Refined cuisine using regional fresh produce. Duck the obvious speciality in Restaurant Endtenfang		
		♫	Music in Cellar Grotte
		£/$	C

Wald-und Schlosshotel Friedrichsruhe

Originally a hunting lodge, rebuilt in its present state in the 18th century, this schloss was a social gathering place for the Counts of Hohenlohe. Nobility from throughout Europe were entertained here and today there are still plenty of festivities.

In 1842 the farm building was used as an inn — the old sign 'Grunes Haus' is displayed in the bar, and around 1845 Friedrichsruhe was the home of Countess von Schwarzenburg-Sondershausen. As a hotel it has been enlarged so be sure to ask for a specific type of room: there is a new building, accommodation in the former farm building with light pine furnishings; or rooms in the castle itself of antique style — Empire, baroque or Biedermeier.

7111 Friedrichsruhe, Germany. ∅ (07941) 7078

47	(mostly double, including suites)	✳	Cultivated holiday appeal
🏨	Year round	℘	Indoor and outdoor swimming pool, tennis court, sauna, 9-hole golf course, plenty of space for walking and cycling
✕	Large menu featuring items like salad of dove breasts, figs in crème de cassis. 18-page wine list		
		♫	No
		£/$	B

Burghotel Götzenburg

The 'Knight with the Iron Fist' — Götz von Berlichingen —
was born here in 1480 and sometimes you have the feeling
he's still around. If you're not familiar with Goethe's early
play about this hero you may better recall that Mark Twain
called him 'The Old German Robin Hood'. But it is the
Goethe play, along with others — some specifically for
children — which are staged annually in July and August in
the castle yard. Brush up on your German if you plan to
attend.

The Götz story is that he preferred horseriding to
schooling so became a warrior — at 22 he was already
involved in Ansbach-Nuremburg conflicts. During the war
of the Bavarian Succession he accidentally lost his right
hand when the Nuremburg cannon was mistakenly aimed at
their allies so that after 1505 he was seen to wear an 'iron
fist' when he fought feuds — always for a third party. No one
knows who made this apparatus or really how it worked but
it can be seen in the castle's small museum. Also on display
is a Roman statue found on the site and a 1591 tankard
showing an Imperial Eagle.

If you shun the modern and like the rustic, this castle is
fun. In the Knights Hall, a massive piece of furniture 400
years old; in the dining room, lamps designed from hunting
rifles. The hotel guest book provides interesting reading and

the kitchen produces tasty food.

Götz, by the way, lived to over 80, spending his last years at Hornberg Castle where he died in 1562. He was buried at Schöntal Monastery, 6 km (4 miles) from Jagsthausen. Burghotel Götzenburg is located not far from Ohringen and 14 km (8½ miles) from Möckmühl.

7109 Jagsthausen, Germany. ✆ (07943) 2222

19	(mostly double)	✳	Rustic fun
🏨	mid Mar–Oct	♪	Bowling alley. Angling and tennis in town
✕	Tasty German food, good wine cellar	♫	Summer plays in the courtyard; medieval meals
		£/$	C

Schlosshotel Grünwald

A former hunting lodge not far from Munich, this schloss is a delightful small place today with a typical Bavarian character. Duke Ludwig the Strict built a fortified castle here in 1293 and the self-proclaimed Emperor Ludwig (his son) spent his youth here. Later, it was the residence of Duke Sigismund.

Grünwald is Munich's fashionable suburb, where everyone comes to drink the young wine. Here at the hotel, that may be done on the garden terrace overlooking the Isar Valley or in the Knights' Hall. The public rooms are full of antiques and carved wooden statues but the bedrooms are more of an eclectic mix.

Grünwald may be reached in a 25 minute streetcar trip from the centre of Munich. From the airport motorway, the correct exit is marked Oberhaching/Grünwald.

Zeillerstrass 1, 8022 Grünwald, Germany.
℘ **(089) 641935**

16	(all individually decorated; all with en suite bathroom and colour TV; mini bar in the suites)	✳	Quietly gemütlich
		℘	River and rock beach within walking distance
🏨	mid Jan–Dec	♫	No
✗	French and Italian cuisine	£/$	B

Schlosshotel Heinsheim

The von Racknitz family have always liked people... entertaining, generation after generation over 350 years, but always in their castle home. So it is not that much of a surprise that they decided to welcome strangers through their door (in the hopes they, too, would soon become friends) in 1951 when Heinsheim became a hotel.

Originally, the family came from Styria but religious pressure forced them to leave. Allowed to sell their possessions by Emperor Ferdinand II in 1628, the family first chose Regensburg and Nuremberg and only later bought Heinsheim where in 1730 the rural baroque castle was built, and enclosed by a large park. Lord of the manor at that time was Karl von Racknitz. He may have been temperamental and drove his coach at manic speed, but it is thanks to him there are so many beautiful old trees in the park today — brought back along with exotic plants from expeditions into Mexico.

Ancestral pictures adorn the walls of the ancestral hall today, side by side with framed petit-point embroideries. No better place to sit than by the open fire, with a glass of Heinsheimer Schwarzriesling to hand. The wine comes from the castle's own vineyard, and is also served in the cellar bar or out on the terrace. The owners put special emphasis on their cuisine — they started off by serving supper with wine in a rustic tavern converted from a stable. Since then, they have become a little more sophisticated without losing any of their country charm.

When the castle became a hotel, the old chambers were modernised and now boast every comfort. Heinsheim is located only 4 km (2½ miles) from the spa of Bad Rappenau and 45 km (28 miles) from Heidelberg.

6927 Bad Rappenau-Heinsheim, Germany.
✆ (07264) 1045

40 (mostly double, some modern, others antique style; all with en suite bathroom and mini bar)	✳ Gemütlichkeit
	℘ Open air swimming pool for summer use in surrounding park. The health resorts of Bad Rappenau and Bad Wimpfen only 4 km (2½ miles) away.
🏨 Feb–mid Dec	
✕ Typical German hearty fare	
	♫ No
	£/$ C

Schlosshotel Hirschhorn

Early in the 13th century, a Knight of Steinach built this fortress at what you can see is a strategic point — just take in the view from the terrace. His son called himself 'von Hirschhorn' — the line was to continue until 1632. One of the most important members of the family was Hans von Hirschhorn, supreme judge of Palatine (for whom one of today's guest rooms is named).

The hotel is so artfully incorporated into the older structure that it scarcely appears to be a hotel at all, but all the rooms are different, comfortable and quiet. The wedding room (No. 4) is particularly richly decorated. The old private chapel is now a TV lounge and the Knights Hall is used for medieval feasts. Look at the alliance coat of arms of Ludwig von Hirschhorn and Maria von Hatzfeld of 1586 at the southern side of the palace, and climb the tower for a few pfennigs. The castle has a pleasant restaurant and its own pastry shop.

6932 Hirschhorn/Neckar, Germany. ✆ (06272) 1373

8	(all double)	✳	Romantic
		℘	No
🏨	Feb–Nov	♫	No
✗	Regional dishes with fish and game the specialities	£/$	C

Burghotel Hornberg

The 'Knight with the Iron Fist', Götz von Berlichingen, was born at what is now Burghotel Götzenburg, but he spent the last years of his life at Hornberg — and died here in 1562. The castle, mind you, was first recorded in 1184 when it belonged to the burgraves of Lauffen. In 1471 Lutz Schott built the large manor opposite the entrance and, in 1510, his son added the palace. When Götz von Berlichingen bought it in 1517, he had spent two years in prison in Augsburg and had to vow never to leave this castle again. Instead, he wrote his life story by dictating it to his priest. During the von Berlichingens' tenure, the building with the Knights Hall and the hexagonal tower were added. In 1612, the scholarly Reinhard von Gemmingen purchased the castle which is now in the 11th generation's possession of that same family.

A medieval atmosphere certainly prevails but the castle complex has been put to good modern use. The sheep's barn is now hotel reception; former stables are the restaurant 'Im alten Marstall'. The Knight's armour is displayed in the 'Götzenstube' and the remarkable door to the wine cellar shows the date 1596.

There are wonderful views across the castle's own vineyards to the Neckar Valley — from the castle terrace, the 'Götzengrill' and from the narrow window niches. Bedrooms have names, not numbers. You could choose the

Gun-powder Chamber, the Treasure Chamber or the Arms' Chamber or opt for upstairs in the tower to the Dovecot, Swallows' Nest or Eagles' Nest. You will find open fireplaces and copper etchings, pewter pieces and murals depicting medieval scenes. You will see museum displays and 16th-century dates and coats of arms. And, of course, there are torch-lit knightly banquets.

Hornberg's management will happily arrange daily fishing cards for guests wishing to angle on the rivers, and will make arrangements for motor boat trips on the Neckar. The surrounding areas are ideal for walking and hiking, including the castle's own forest. Hornberg is located 13 km (8 miles) from the spa of Bad Rappenau whose facilities include a heated swimming pool with artificial waves and an indoor brine pool, and 7 km (4½ miles) from the town of Mosbach, noted for its Franconian-style timbered buildings.

6951 Neckarzimmern, Germany. ✆ (06261) 4064

27 (mostly double, including tower rooms; almost all with private bathroom, some with mini bar, some with balcony)

🏨 Mar–Nov

✗ The 'schlupfnudeln' noodles are famous. Also recommended: the 'Schlemmerplatte' comprising veal, pork and hare with fresh mushrooms and Bernaise sauce. Accompanied of course by Hornberg's own wines like Götzhalde and Wallmauer.

✳ Medieval enough to be fascinating; modern enough to be very comfortable

🌳 No hotel facilities but plenty of sports possibilities nearby, including tennis, riding, flying and swimming. Arrangements easily made for fishing or boating trips

♫ Medieval banquets and spit-roast barbecues

£/$ C

Hotel Schloss Hugenpoet

Any hotel with the offputting name of 'Toad pool' (which is what 'Hugenpoet' means) has to make up for it somehow and this lovely 16th-century moated castle certainly does. It has been praised for service (more than two members of staff to every one guest) and for its cuisine (guests with gastronomic know-how are appreciated), which is why it is Michelin-rosette-rated. It stands close to the Ruhr's industry yet you never feel it, for its location is in a wooded valley by the river, a green island of tranquillity.

The Barons of Nesselrode first built a castle on this site in the 14th century only to see it razed during a feud in 1478. A new castle was erected close by in 1509 but suffered such great damage during the Thirty Years' War that it was pulled down in 1647, making way for the present structure (1650). The Nesselrodes continued to rule Hugenpoet until debts forced a sale to Baron Friedrich Leopold von Fürstenberg in 1831. During the next decade it was enlarged and provided with its own water supply and by 1879 it was the Fürstenberg family's permanent residence. The castle became a hotel in 1955 under a leased contract with the Fürstenbergs.

Hugenpoet is littered with antiques and fine paintings and has a particularly handsome black marble staircase from 1696 in its entrance hall, but most noteworthy of all are its fireplaces. Sculpted of Kalkar stone, they are magnificent works of Renaissance art. Look at the one facing the staircase depicting the fate of Lot; the one in the yellow salon whose central motif shows the mourning of Abel's death; and the one in the red salon. Probably the most exquisite one of all is to be found in the green salon, dating from 1578 and portraying the flight from Troy.

Bedrooms are furnished with period pieces as one might expect — the four poster in No. 12 is 400 years old — but, oddly, the dining room is very modern, light and airy. Food is French in style and presentation; specialities are listed on a 'Menu Dégustation'. Dining here is meant to be an experience — it is not the place to ask for beans on toast! An exceptionally good wine list concentrates on only the best of German wines and features many French varieties.

Situated between Essen and Kettwig (where the Krupp family home is now a museum), Hugenpoet is easily reached by motorway. There is a tennis court in the castle park and other sport possibilities nearby, but the main attraction is the food.

4300 Essen 18 (Kettwig), August-Thyssen-Strasse 51, Germany. ✆ **(02054) 6054**

21	(mostly double, some with original 16th-century furniture; all with en suite bathroom, TV and mini bar)	✳	Prestigious. Cared for, gourmet orientated. Not a child's first choice
🏰	Year round	℘	Tennis court in castle park. Nearby golf course, riding and swimming pools
✕	Foodies rate it number one. Superb if you like French menus with suggestions like chanterelle with fried goose liver. No one knocks the wines—21 pages worth of the best, including pricey valuables	♫	No
		£/$	B

Schlosshotel Kommende Ramersdorf

At first glance you might think Kommende is going to be an extremely noisy place to stay — it's ringed by a motorway, after all. In reality it's no such thing — guest rooms are in a side wing, sufficiently quiet for only birdsong to filter through.

The castle was donated by Count Heinrich III von Sayn around 1220 and for many centuries after belonged to the Teutonic Order. The present main building was erected during the time of the Grand Master and Elector, Clemens August, using parts of the medieval construction. When Napoléon confiscated the schloss, the duchy of Berg sold it to the princes of Salm-Reifferscheid-Dyck who were succeeded by the barons of Francq and von Oppenheim. The latter had the house remodelled in the last part of the 19th century in the fashion of the time, as you'll note from the coloured ceiling framework and wooden wall coverings.

Much of Kommende has in fact become a museum displaying hand-polished early Victorian and baroque furniture and rustic oak German fitments from the 18th century. The proprietors, themselves, are antique dealers so they not only knowledgeably point out that rosewood writing desk here or that ebony and ivory cabinet there, but sell a number of the antiques on view to fanciers.

Antique furniture (not for sale) decorates the guest rooms.

Buffet breakfasts are taken in the bright and colourful breakfast room, but there is also a Viennese-style café from whose terrace you can see the spires of Bonn and the Rhine Valley surrounding it. The main restaurant is far more baroque and oddly enough specialises in Italian cuisine. Kommende is located within a 10 minute drive of Bonn and 20 minutes of Cologne airport.

5300 Bonn 3 (Beuel), Oberkasseler Strasse 10, Germany. ✆ (0228) 440734

18	(10 double, 8 single, all with en suite bathroom, some with colour TV. Rates include buffet breakfast)	✳	Museumy
		℘	No, but all sport facilities nearby
		♫	No
		£/$	C
🏨	Year round		
✗	Good Italian food		

Hotel Klostergut Jakobsberg

This is a case of a large former monastery becoming a larger-than-usual hotel that offers everything in the way of sports. The monastery was founded in 1157 by Barbarossa, so called because of his red beard though his correct title was Emperor Friedrich I, — for both monks and nuns. Every year they sent a cart-load of wine from the imperial vineyards of Boppard, as is witnessed by a 1262 document signed by King Richard of Cornwall acknowledging the tribute.

However, it was difficult to remain solvent in those times and neither the chapter of Trier who owned the domain in the early 16th century, nor the zu Liebenstein inheritors who bought it all in 1599, could make ends meet, so in 1640 it was sold to the Jesuits of Koblenz. When Pope Clement XIV dissolved the Jesuit Order the property was turned into a school, later passed into private ownership and was eventually purchased by a Bonn manufacturer in 1960.

Kostergut's range of recreational facilities is far more important these days than its heritage, though only use of the indoor pool is free to the overnight guest. (Special packages are available which emphasise food, or include tennis with instruction, weekend rates, etc.) Still, you can name your game otherwise: tennis — indoors and out, squash, skeet, bowling, riding, hunting, walking. Guests who want to be pampered may opt for a sauna and a host of different massages or the sunbed.

For the most part, the décor at this hotel is modern though those with an eye for artwork will find that, too. Plenty of Benetton's work in wrought iron, especially in the inner court decorated with huge copper kettle flower stands once used for sugar making. Hotel corridors are enhanced by hundreds of pictures, engravings and lithographs. If some of them are of balloons, it's because the Bonn purchaser was a hot-air balloonist and it was his idea to name one of the bars, the Montgolfier, after those brothers who hot-air ballooned in 1783. The owner's collection of pipes and tobacco boxes is an interesting one and his collection of hunting rifles and shotguns is also on display along with trophies of all kinds — among them, the antlers from a Hungarian stag that reached world record length.

Where the monks once stored their wine is now the Safari Bar, which like the Jakobsstube has a trophy or two. But the Charollais cattle bred on the grounds here are for more practical purposes.

Klostergut Jakobsberg looms over the Rhine, though its rooms and terrace unfortunately face the wrong way for a panoramic view. Delightful Boppard is very close and easy excursions may be made into Koblenz.

5407 Boppard/Rhein, Germany. ✆ (06742) 3061

110	(102 are double; all with bathroom en suite, TV and mini bar).	✱	First class for family sport enthusiasts, but somewhat conference group orientated
🏨	Year round		
✗	International. Look out for Japanese Chitaki mushrooms on the menu— recommended especially with loin of veal in goose-liver mousse. Diet menus can be arranged	♂	Excellent. Indoor swimming pool, sauna, solarium, variety of massages, tennis (indoor and out), squash, bowling, table tennis, billiards, garden chess, skeet and trap. Hunting and riding may be arranged. Heliport
		♫	No
		£/$	C

Schlosshotel Kronberg

Such a towered and gabled, greenish grey edifice as this is, is without doubt, awe inspiring. It was built for Kaiser Friedrich III's widow — the Empress Frederick, Queen Victoria's eldest daughter. Designed and embellished by her, it stands today as a monument to her husband, a reminder of the world they had hoped to create together — albeit now an outstandingly classy hotel.

Ernst Eberhard von Ihne architected the castle with elements of German Renaissance, Tudor Gothic and local half-timbered style. The Empress filled it with books and paintings, tapestries and porcelains, surrounding herself with as much beauty as possible to combat the time of her life that was the most sad. For by 1889, having had to wait out 30 years, Emperor Freidrich III had died after only 99 days reign. His successor son, Wilheim II (the Kaiser) wouldn't allow his mother to keep her favourite home at Potsdam so she chose here, Kronberg, at the foot of the Taunus for her retreat, one she was only able to enjoy for seven years before her death in 1901.

Kronberg has become an exclusive meeting place for international society, starred for excellence of service, but in many ways it is a museum piece. The heavy wooden-ceilinged hall alone permeates a stately air and, at the top of the stairs, a priceless Gobelin tapestry takes attention. The wood-panelled bar, modern enough, has genuine Turners and Reynolds on its walls. The large dining room seems very grand with its woodwork, high ceilings and huge Dutch marble fireplace.

Rooms that are used for private functions these days are worth peeking into for their décor: The Blue Salon, Louis-Seize room with wooden panelling from the Russian Court in Frankfurt and the Louis-Quatorze-style Green Salon decorated with full length portraits. One of the loveliest rooms is The Library where a Flemish chandelier hangs from the coffered ceiling. Glass cabinets in the hall and octagonal small dining room hold smaller treasures: Venetian glasses, Limoges enamels.

The Empress' English childhood is reflected in the very 'English' park surrounding the castle with its rose gardens and, these days, an 18-hole golf course. Very pleasant for a peaceful walk any time of year. No wonder the aristocrats loved it here — King Edward VII, Czar Nicholas II, King Christian IX of Denmark and King Umberto I of Italy. Today's guests pay for the privilege but rates aren't super royal, no more than the leading hotels of Frankfurt, 17 km (10½ miles) away.

6242 Kronberg/Taunus, Haistrasse 25, Germany.
✆ (06173) 7011

55	(single, double, suites and royal suites, all with en suite facilities and colour TV)	✳	Ornate, grandly Victorian
		℘	18-hole golf course on the castle grounds. Swimming and tennis available in Kronberg
▦	Year round		
✗	Excellent quality, superb setting. Sample items: breast of pigeon with potato truffle salad, roast quail with lentils, calf's sweetbreads on a leek fondue	♫	No
		£/$	B

Schlosshotel Kurfürstliches Amtshaus

Several fortifications have stood on this site in the volcanic Eifel mountain landscape, but the hotel as it is today is an enlarged and renovated version of a comfortable hunting castle built in 1712.

The hotel appears to be full of clocks: in glass display cases and in the Grafenschenke bar. Décor is an excellent mix of old and new: rooms have modern comforts but also some antique furniture. Actually the most famous bed was made in the 1950s of solid oak for the Federal Republic's guesthouse and some 52 crowned and uncrowned heads have spent a night in it.

Haute cuisine is featured in the dining room where one can admire the painting of Empress Maria Theresa and a 17th-century French wine cabinet.

The castle is 8 km (5 miles) from the centre of Daun.

5568 Daun/Eifel, Auf dem Burgberg, Germany.
✆ (06592) 303133

42	(mostly double, some four posters)	✳	Modernly comfortable
🏨	Year round	℘	Swimming pool, sauna and solarium. Other sports in town
✗	Inspired combinations like mussels in coriander and olive sauce	♬	By special arrangement
		£/$	C

Schlosshotel Lembeck

Looking at this fortified, moated, baroque-style castle, situated on two islets in the middle of a lake, you could think it offers more accommodation than it does. Only six rooms are available for rent, charming though they are with period furniture and modern conveniences, sloping floors and original beams.

Lembeck's history dates back to the 12th century though the present building was constructed between 1670 and 1692. The museum on the first floor still shows the original colours of its beamed ceiling and the fireplace with its colourful coat of arms is dated 1563. Of particular beauty are the Biedermeier room and Rasefeld's 1610 four poster bed. On the second floor, a modern gallery displays HH Merveldt's paintings.

Lembeck village is only 1½ km (1 mile) or so away and the town of Dorsten, 13 km (8 miles).

4270 Dorsten 12 (Lembeck), Germany. ☏ (02369) 7213

6	(all with period décor, some four posters; all with private bathroom)	✳	Intimate, cosy
		℘	Swimming and riding in Lembeck
▦	Year round but not Mon	♫	Disco
✕	Typical Westphalian fare	£/$	C

Hotel Jagdschloss Niederwald

A perfect situation — high above Rüdesheim in an oasis of quiet, surrounded by a national park and yet easy to reach from the Rhine-Main area — makes this hotel a popular business as well as holiday base. The original hunting castle on this site was built by Maximilian von Ostein in 1764 and became the estate of the Dukes of Nassau in 1835, who then turned the 'Niederwald' into a park. This has since become the nature park, Rheingau-Untertaunus. The castle itself was destroyed by fire but reconstructed in the 1920s, following original plans, and opened as a hotel in 1929. It was here in 1948 that the Federal Republic of Germany was born when Konrad Adenauer met with prime ministers from the other states, in the Green Salon.

If you're not looking for dungeons and suits of armour but rather enjoy tasteful and relaxing surroundings, you've found the right place. From the glass-enclosed verandah on the northern side, a peaceful view of the meadows and hills. In good weather, sit under the plane trees on the south terrace for a coffee or meal.

Management prides itself on its personal touch, filling the hotel with fresh flowers and advising guests on food and the famous wines of the Rheingau. They also pride themselves on their sports facilities: a pleasantly heated indoor pool, sauna and solarium, well kept all-weather tennis courts.

Walks and hiking trails start at the front door and lead through woods and vineyards to places where Goethe and Beethoven liked to stroll.

Sightseers won't have to be urged to get out into the Rheingau region with its wine villages and castles, take a boat cruise on the Rhine, visit the wine vaults of the Trockenbeerenauslesegruft. Jagdschloss Niederwald is located 5 km (3 miles) from the railway station at Rüdesheim and a 45 minute drive from Frankfurt airport.

6220 Rüdesheim/Rhein, Germany. ∅ (06722) 1004

52	(mostly double, all with en suite bathroom, colour TV)	✳	Peaceful modern
		℘	Indoor pool, sauna,
🏫	Mar–Nov		solarium. Two all-weather
✕	Classical French with		tennis courts, walking and
	emphasis on fresh produce.		hiking trails, riding.
	Specialities include game		Recreation area in
	and wild poultry. Excellent		Rüdesheim
	wine list for Rheingau	♫	No
	wines, from Riesling to	£/$	B
	Assmannshauser red		

Hotel Schloss Petershagen

This former residence of the Prince-bishops of Minden was converted into a most attractive hotel in 1964 — small, comfortable with recommendable service. Its history pre-dates Columbus' discovery of America for it was in 1306 that Bishop Gotffried von Waldeck decided to build a castle here. Various bishops were in residence until 1650 and during the Thirty Years' War, both invited guests and the uninvited like General Tilly and King Christian of Denmark, found themselves under its roof.

At the end of that war when the Minden diocese was annexed by Prussia, the Great Elector of Mark Brandenburg came to the castle to receive homage from the Minden estates. In 1799, King Friedrich Wilhelm and his queen were guests here. Petershagen has seen splendid occasions and those which have been grim like the burning of the witches in the castle moat at the end of the dark Middle Ages. Nowadays you will find the hotel a peaceful retreat on the banks of the River Weser.

As a hotel it is a pleasant combination of old and new: antique furniture and engravings, a wooden statue of a buttoned, gaitered dragoon holding court in the Count Palatine dining room, yet pretty wallpaper and light furnishings for the terrace room overlooking the river. The former bishops' dressing room has become a bar and all the guest rooms have private bath.

Petershaven is located 12 km (7½ miles) from Minden.

4953 Petershagen/Weser, Schlossstrasse 5–7,
Germany. ✆ (05707) 346

11	(mostly double, all with private bathroom)	✳	Restful
🏨	Mar–Dec	♪	Heated outdoor pool, tennis
✗	Mushrooms galore: fresh with a herb sauce, cream of chanterelles with chervil, fish with oyster mushrooms	♫	No
		£/$	C

Dornroschenschloss Sababurg

Sleeping beauties in their right minds bring their prince with them to this castle since kissing guests is not part of the staff house rules! Sababurg, however, is the setting for that most famous fairy tale written by the Brothers Grimm who were frequent visitors. It has the setting, in the heart of the Reinhard Forest, that is perfect for fairy stories but this make-believe world comes complete with modern comforts, even if they do keep the fables alive with summertime 'fairytale' banquets.

This is the land of heresay and you may hear all sorts of accounts as to how the castle acquired its name 'Sababurg', but it is likely it derived from 'Zappenborgk' as it was known in the 14th century. Be it fact or fiction, a miraculous religious discovery in nearby Gottsburen led to the building of a fortification in 1334 to safeguard the avalanche of pilgrims who descended on the area. A dispute over ownership resulted in half the castle belonging to Mainz, half to Hessen, until 1429 when Hessen took over the lot. Left to fall into disrepair, by 1455 the 'Zappenborgk' was deserted. But Count Wilhelm I who hunted here built a new hunting castle on the site, one which was soon to host splendid banquets for visitors from the court of Kassel.

In 1571 Wilhelm IV extended the castle and added what is now the world's oldest game park. Not only was this count a statesman but a prominent scientist, too, with the idea of keeping and breeding unfamiliar animals for research purposes. Reindeer arrived from the Swedish court; black deer were sent by Duke Julius of Brunswick; red deer from Albrecht of Bavaria. A thick rose hedge and then a wall was erected to protect them. Nowadays, this game park helps to preserve and recreate the big game once so abundant in Europe's great forests. Nowadays, your guest room overlooks wild horses and bison who roam the spacious, walled grounds.

Though looted and damaged during the Thirty Years' War and the Seven Years' War, not to mention natural hazards, Sababurg was magnificently restored by Friedrich II in 1765. Once again there were parties and stylish guest rooms with animal pictures on their doors. Between then and now, the wooden sections were demolished and changes made, but in 1961 the castle took on a new lease of life. Today, you will still retire to an individually named bedroom — 'Das Einhorn' (The Unicorn). 'Im Wildt' (The Game) or 'In der wilden Sau' (The Wild Sow) perhaps. You will dine on lordly game in the dining room or torch-lit castle ruins, take tea on a terrace overlooking the oak forest.

Sababurg is located 12 km (7½ miles) from the railway station of Hofgeismar and 35 km (22 miles) from Kassel where there is a Brothers Grimm Museum. It's good walking country around the castle — in 20 minutes you can reach the primeval forest where ferns reach man's height and the giant trees may be 600 to 800 years old.

3520 Hofgeismar (Sababurg), Germany. ✆ (05678) 1052

18	(mostly twin, all with bathroom)	✳	Straight out of a fairy book
🏰	Mar–Dec	℘	Sauna and solarium in the hotel. The game park and
✕	Specialities are spit roasts, game and fresh fish from the forest streams		vicinity has marked paths for walking
		♫	'Fairytale' banquets
		£/$	C

Der Schafhof

When you see this lovely little hotel you'll agree that the Church always chose enchanting spots for their monastery estates. This one belonged to the Amorbach Benedictine Abbey. Records show a domain stood here in 1446 and even today you can see the date 1574, when Theobald Garmblich was abbot to the monastery, carved on the corner beam of the old barn. The main building of the Shafhof, as seen today, was built in 1723 of red sandstone.

In 1974 Der Shafhof was in a bad state of repair but thanks to the purchase and renovation by the Winklers, who turned it into a hotel, it once again has charm and atmosphere. Rural baroque? Some people describe it so. Rustic luxury? For sure. It's not unknown to discover a flock of sheep on the doorstep! The guest rooms are what you might expect of a country place modernised for comfort — sloping beamed ceilings, wooden furniture, a four poster in No. 17. Beds made up with snowy linen; private bathrooms.

Der Shafhof prides itself on its cuisine, based on produce from its own farm — anything from its breakfast jams to its lunch time cider and after dinner fruit brandies. There's the friendly family setting of the Pilgerstube or Shaferstube and the country elegance of the Abstube.

The peaceful location on a slope of wood and meadow by the village of Amorbach is perfect for riding and walking in the nearby woods and generally exploring the area. Frankfurt is 85 km (53 miles) away.

14   (mostly double, 2 suites, 1 four poster, all with en suite bathroom)

🏨 mid Feb–early Jan

✗ Plenty of lamb and trout from the Der Shafhof farm. Home-made plum jams, cider and fruit brandies from their own distillery

❋ Rural baroque

🎾 All-weather tennis court. Other sports at Amorbach

🎵 No

£/$ C

Burghotel Schnellenberg

In a wooded setting an hour's drive from Frankfurt stands Westphalia's mightiest fortress and one of Germany's finest castle hotels. Schnellenberg was fortified in 1222 by Cologne's Archbishop Engelbert von Berg in order to secure one of the most important trading routes in the Sauerland — 'Heidenstrasse'. In 1291, Johann von Plettenberg, marshal of the duchy of Westphalia, strengthened the place even more though by 1333 the lords Vogt von Elspe had taken over ownership.

The castle's golden age began in 1594 when Caspar von Fürstenberg bought it, as you will see if you take the time to look at the old chapel. The altar and the Prince-Bishop's throne are of marble and alabaster and other furnishings are of elaborately carved wood. Much of the core of what you see today dates from the 17th century despite a 19th-century fire which destroyed roofs and the interior. Caspar von Fürstenberg's coat of arms is on the gate tower and his motto seems most appropriate for today's offered hospitality: 'Stranger, don't stay outside, my door is wide open for the traveller'.

Other coats of arms decorate the cellar bar, appropriately a bar since a brewery was housed here in the past. The oldest part of the castle is the upper section where rooms have stuccoed beamed ceilings, quite a rarity. In some of the rooms, like No. 70, the beams have purposely been left visible.

What used to be the stable now contains a museum with rare items like a 1600 cross-bow and a 17th-century almanac. Another noticeable piece is a travel cabinet with porcelains.

Scenic surroundings are suited to outdoor sports: swimming in Lake Biggesee, rowing, fishing and riding. A special 'Knights for 5 days' package is a hotel feature.

5952 Attendom am Biggesee, Germany. ✆ (02722) 6940

42	(mostly double, including tower rooms, all with en suite bathroom, TV and room bar)	✳	Lordly but informal
		♟	Schnellenberg has its own bowling alley and tennis court. Swimming is possible in Lake Biggesee. Riding and fishing available in the area
🏰	Feb–Dec		
✕	Hearty German		
		♫	No
		£/$	C

Burghotel auf Schönburg

Auf Schönburg, perched high over the Rhine, is part of a 1000-year-old castle, built by a local Oberwesel family. Back in the 14th century some 250 people lived here and there were probably 24 co-owners of its stables, cellars, warehouses and great halls. After being burnt by the French in 1689, the castle remained a ruin for two centuries, albeit a remarkable one as Victor Hugo pointed out. Though the estate changed hands several times, it wasn't until a German American invested in its restoration that what you see today began to reappear. In the 1950s the town purchased it and the hotel opened its doors.

From below, the fortified walls seem a little grim, but in reality this family-run hotel is very friendly. Because it is part of the castle, you'll discover narrow passages leading to secret chambers from which to view the lush Rhine valley. Such guest rooms as the small beamed one on the parapet walk with its canopied bed and old spinning wheel, or No. 23 in the tower, are delightfully cosy, though No. 13 probably has the best view of all — across Oberwesel, the Pfalz and the islet of Kaub. A stay here is like living a fable.

Both the Erker Gaststübe and the Knappenstübe dining rooms have a gemütlich (sense of well being) atmosphere and in good weather you can enjoy your glass of Sieben-Jungfrauen-Rieslingspätlese wine in the small open air courtyard. This is the perfect castle hotel base for exploring what for many is the most picturesque section of the Rhine.

6532 Oberwessel/Rhein, Germany. ✆ (06744) 7027

22	(mostly double, all with private facilities)	✳	Warm and friendly
🏨	Mar–Nov. Restaurant closed Mon	⚲	Not on site but many sports nearby at St Goar
✗	High quality German	♫	No
		£/$	C

Burghotel Schwalenberg

Burghotel Schwalenberg has been a convalescent home and a children's home so it almost seems appropriate that it should be a German 'home from home' for holidaymakers. But naturally, all this is 20th-century background — the castle itself dates to the 13th when Count Wolkwin III of Schwalenberg built it and founded the town.

Not that this count was a gentle man even though he did hold a high office. Both he and his brother were robber knights and participated in the murder of Archbishop Engelbert of Cologne. However, sins are invariably found out and, as atonement, the brothers were obliged to build the Monastery of Mariental near Netze, in Waldeck, and the Monastery of Falkenhagen (where Wolkwin was eventually buried in 1249).

As a reminder of those terrible times you will find a cannon in the reception area, scattered suits of armour and murderous weapons. There are saints, too: on the first floor and in the Knights Hall where gilded bishops watch over guests.

Centuries of turmoil almost led to the destruction of this castle in the centre of Lippe land until it was restored for Princess Friederike zur Lippe at the beginning of this century. Since 1971 it has been operated as a family-run castle hotel. Where once one might have feared for one's life, there is convivial atmosphere and latterday comforts. In the Knights Room bar, old rifles merely serve as partition decorations between the seating booths, and the armoured knight next to the hotel piano just maintains a stern countenance to ensure weekend guests do get up and dance.

Spacious guest rooms are perhaps more modern than one would care to find in a castle, but then again a private bathroom and a mini bar is often very welcome even if the ceilings aren't beamed and vaulted. The view from the restaurant's large windows is of picturesque Schwalenberg village below, and nearby lakes and rivers provide fresh fish for the menu.

Schwalenberg is located not far from the spas of Bad Pyromont, Bad Meinberg and Bad Driburg and offers special 'Knight of the Castle' packages which include a medieval feast.

4938 Schieder-Schwalenberg 2, Germany.
℘ (05284) 5167

---

19 (mostly double, including a four poster, all with en suite bathroom and mini bar)	✳ Friendly and fun
	℘ Arrangements can be made for covered wagon tours through the Schwalenberger Wald, sailing, canoeing and swimming on the Emmer reservoir. Riding, golf and tennis facilities not far away
🏨 Mar–Dec	
✗ Fresh trout and, thanks to the proprietors, Swabian dishes like 'Maultaschen' and 'Spätzle', both noodle specialities	
	♫ Piano music and dancing
	£/$ C

Hotel zum Schwan

In 1818 this former hunting lodge was an inn and it is again, today. It was built in beautifully baroque style by Landgrave Friedrich II von Hessen-Cassel, son of the founder of the equally delightful town, in 1760. His father, Carl von Hessen-Cassel, conceived the notion for the harbour where today only swans swim, and on his orders famous city architect du Rhy created the town's classic style. From the hotel terrace you can look out on to that old harbour, or relax in the garden surroundings.

Zum Schwan has been in the same family hands for three generations. Latterday owners have modernised guest rooms, but the exquisite rococo hall that is now the candle-lit restaurant has been completely preserved as it was.

3522 Bad Karlshafen, Conradistrasse 3–4, Germany.
✆ (05672) 1044

31	(20 double, 11 single, all modern with en suite bathroom, colour TV and video and mini bar)	✳	Friendly and charming
		℘	Canoeing on the Weser, riding, mini golf and mineral baths in Bad Karlshafen
🏨	Year round		
✗	Local game, French fresh poultry, Atlantic fish	♫	No
		£/$	C

Hotel Schloss Spangenberg

Long before you reach the small town where it is located you will see the castle of Spangenberg — one of the finest fortifications in Hesse, standing on a hilltop looking just the way a medieval château should.

Among the various owners there were three important landgraves: Otto 'the marksman' (1322–1367), a keen hunter who lived here as a co-sovereign, Ludwig I 'the pacifist' (1413–1458) who, it is said, refused the crown because he had no wish to leave his home country, and Philipp 'the magnanimous' (1509–1567) who introduced the Reformation into Hesse.

The castle's outer walls were erected in the 17th century — tunnels from the arsenal lead to them. Spangenberg was not conquered during the Thirty Years' War but was taken by the French for the first time during the Seven Years' War in the 18th century. It has been a prison: for the French in 1870 and for English officers in World War II.

3509 Spangenberg, Germany. ✆ (05663) 866

24	(all with en suite bathroom)	✳	Comfortable
🏨	Feb–Dec	ᛰ	No, but several sports in town
✕	Game specialities	♫	No
		£/$	C

Hotel Schloss Thiergarten

Now an exclusive small hotel on the outskirts of Bayreuth, Thiergarten was built as a hunting castle in 1716 for Georg Wilhelm to a design by Johann David Rantz. The stucco was done by Domenico Cadenazzi. You can't miss the hunting connection — a huge elk and other trophies regard diners in the Fireplace Restaurant; the chandelier overlooking the staircase is made of carved wooden antlers; and the octagonal, dome-shaped hall is decorated with well-preserved stuccoes showing hunting motifs. Some people say game was driven into this hall and shot from the galleries above.

Guest rooms are named for the margraves hunting areas — the Kaiserhammer is popular with the romantic. Afternoon coffee may be taken on the terrace or in the mirrored Venetian Salon.

8580 Bayreuth, Oberthiergartener Strasse 36, Germany. ✆ (09209) 1314

8	(all double)	✳	Exclusive
		℘	Own sauna, but other
🏨	Year round		sports in Bayreuth
✗	Nouvelle cuisine type	♫	No
		£/$	C

Burg Trendelburg

Built by Konrad III of Schoneberg in 1300, the castle was documented under different names in different years: Trindirberg in 1303 but Dredeneburg in 1305, Drederburg in 1378 and not until 1644 was it known as Trendelburgk. During the 14th century, the castle belonged to no single person but had sections of it sold or pawned to pay debts or pledges. Landgrave Ludwig von Hessen became the owner in 1429 and, after two fires, bailiff Hans von Stoghusen is mentioned as lord of the castle. More fires were to come during the early 17th century and later even though by this time Trendelburg was more a princely hunting lodge than a fortress.

After the Seven Years' War, Trendelburg was used to house invalids, then the revenue office and court justice and later was rented to foresters and road supervisors. Little was done to preserve it until 1900 when Col. von Stockhausen purchased it and helped shape it into what you see today. It was one of the first German castles to be converted to a hotel in 1949 when Hans-Ludwig von Stockhausen, released from a Russian prison, returned here to open a family hotel.

Since then, bathrooms have been artfully installed in the unlikeliest of places—in the wedding tower room, guests have to walk through a wardrobe to reach it! This room, reserved for newlyweds (though the tower has been a prison in the past) is one of the best with an 18th-century four poster bed. The former chapel has become an unusual dining room though there's more space in the Knights Hall and splendid views from the terrace.

3526 Trendelburg 1, Germany. ✆ (05675) 1021

22	(mostly double, furnished in period style with cleverly incorporated bathrooms)	✳	Medieval charm
		℘	Not on site, but many sports in Trendelburg
🏨	mid Feb–early Jan	♫	No
✗	Menu includes castle specialities like 'Shoneberger Grafenvesper'	£/$	C

Hotel Schloss Vellberg

High above the lovely Buhler valley perches this gem of a castle hotel. As a fortification, it was first recorded in 1102, remaining constantly in von Vellberg family hands until 1523. After it was destroyed by the Swabian Confederation it was reconstructed in its present Renaissance style in 1543.

You can see that the irregular and unique relay-gable-construction from the 16th century dominates the outer frame of the house. The Knights Hall, used for banquets, has 16th-century wall paintings and there are well-preserved frescoes from that era in the chapel.

Guest rooms are in the old barracks but rather more comfortable than in Napoléonic times. Honeymooners opt for the City Gate Tower which guards the whole of the rock and is ideal for those not wishing to be disturbed. The restaurant is housed in the former armoury.

7175 Vellberg, Germany. ✆ (07907) 700104

35	(mostly double, all with en suite bathroom)	✳	Favourite choice for honeymooners
🏨	Year round	℘	Sauna, tennis. Other sports in town
✕	Speciality meals include flambéed meats		No
		£/$	C

Burghotel Schloss Waldeck

Landmark of the Waldeck holiday area, this castle once belonged to the Counts of Waldeck whose reign lasted close to 500 years. The still existing north wing dates from the 15th century. By 1665, the castle was no longer a residence and in 1745 it was used to store records (the national archive). After this its principal use was a gaol as you can see from the framed regulations of 1857 which tell prisoners what is expected of them.

Weldeck has been a hotel since 1906 and features an unsparing amount of wood in its reception and function rooms. Rooms look out over the Edersee or the village and the castle cuisine is typically German. To take a look at previous times, visit the dungeon and the castle museum with a kitchen that dates to the Middle Ages. The castle is located about two hours' drive from Frankfurt airport.

3544 Waldeck/Edersee, Germany. ✆ (05623) 5324

11	(9 double, 2 single, all with en suite bathroom)	✳	Established charm
🏨	mid Mar–Oct	℘	No, but plenty to do on Lake Edersee — water skiing, windsurfing, sailing, fishing, etc.
✕	Game and fish from the Edersee		
		♫	Special arrangements include Knights' Feasts
		£/$	C

Parkhotel Wasserburg Anholt

Surrounded by water, park and gardens, the moated castle of Anholt couldn't want for a more romantic setting. In the 12th century this was a fortified site — parts of the still visible walls of the main castle are 13th- and 14th-century. Much of what you see today, such as the main portal, were constructed in the 17th century when the castle was made more comfortable.

World War II damage necessitated a great deal of restoration work so that Wasserburg lacks the medieval atmosphere of other German castle hotels, though the rustic former stable, now a bar, is gemütlich enough. And Wasserburg's museum should not be missed. The premises are beautiful: the Knights' Hall, parade hall, dining rooms and heavy oak carved staircase. A unique picture collection includes Rembrandt's 'Diana and Acteon' along with Dutch masters such as Breughel.

4294 Isselburg Kleverstrasse, Germany. ✆ **(02874) 2044**

29	(including a suite and four poster room, and tower room with own staircase, all with private facilities)	✳	Gracious
		℘	9-hole golf course, cycle rental
🏨	Year round	♫	No
✕	Broiled specialities	£/$	C

Hotel Schloss Weitenburg

If you like the idea of a baronial home that is still a baronial home, Schloss Weitenburg's the place for you. High above the Neckar Valley, between the Black Forest and the Swabian hills, this castle has been converted into a sumptuous hotel by a descendent of the Barons of Rassler.

First mention of a fortified castle here was recorded in 1062; the oldest part to be seen today dates from 1585. Renaissance-styled side wings were added in 1660 and a New Gothic southern wing in 1869. Until 1720 when the Rasslers purchased it, it changed hands many times—at one time owned by the Duke of Württemberg, at another by the Marchtal Monastery.

Robber knights may have lived here back in the 15th century, but today you'll neither feel robbed of comfort nor of value for money. The present Baron only modernised where he felt it was necessary so souvenirs from past centuries adorn the public and guest bedrooms. Hunting trophies and antlers, an 18th-century fire pump and leather water buckets, display cases of glasses, antique chests.

Some of the antiques have been put to especially good use like the wardrobes in rooms No. 1 and 4 which have become bathrooms. Others are simply there for heritage's sake like the 1660 gate, once the castle entrance. Drinks can be taken on a terrace overlooking the valley and meals in a large and interesting dining room.

Ample grounds suit the sporting enthusiast: there's a riding school, 18-hole golf course and plenty of walking paths.

7245 Weitenburg, Germany. ✆ (07457) 8051

35	(mostly double, almost all with private facilities)
🏨	Year round, except 24/25 Dec
✕	Venison soup and other delights

✳	Active baronial home
♆	Indoor pool, sauna and solarium. In the castle grounds there are keep fit trails, stables (riding lessons available) and an 18-hole golf course
♫	No
£/$	C

Schloss Wilkinghege

This schloss was first mentioned in 1311, one of many properties belonging to the von Rhemen zu Barenfeld family. Today's Renaissance style was introduced in 1550 by the Stevenick family and added to in 1719 by Gottfried Pictorius for Herr von Habe and his wife Katharina von Kappel. (Note the double coat of arms above the entrance.) Eventually the castle returned to von Rhemen zu Barenfeld hands until the line became extinct and the present owner bought — and turned Wilkinghege into a hotel.

Despite a 1958 fire, much of the castle character is retained as you'll see from the decorated stucco ceilings, the oil paintings and old engravings. Service, like the décor, is tasteful and discreet.

Wilkinghege is located on the outskirts of Munster which has many interesting churches and museums.

4400 Münster, Steinfurter Strasse 374, Germany.
✆ (0251) 213045

38	(mostly double, all with en suite bathroom, TV and mini bar)	✳	Cultivated discreet elegance, attention to detail
🏨	Year round	♂	9-hole golf course and 6 tennis courts adjacent
✕	Good standard of German food and extensive wine list	♫	No
		£/$	C

Schloss Zell

It is often amazing how a castle becomes a hotel. In 1948, when Schloss Zell was a somewhat rundown property, the owners decided to open a poorly furnished tavern to help keep things going. Along with the wine, there had to be something to eat, they thought — and bread and ham was on the menu. The next year, the first guest rooms had hot and cold running water. And it was at this time that it was discovered that the hen house was in fact a small chapel with lovely Gothic arches. Since then, no one's looked back.

The original fortification was erected in 1543 and the oldest part of the castle is what has become a hotel. That does mean lots of crooked steps and thresholds, enough to make one think twice about that very last glass of Moselle! The vineyards — Zeller Schwarze Katz — by the way have been in the Bohn family for hundreds of years and this wine (Black Cat) has made the quaint little Moselle town of Zell, famous. An ancestor had registered the growth and today it is well consumed in the restaurant, or indeed in the front garden's wine-loggia.

You'll be greeted by Pope Urban, the vintners' patron saint, the moment you enter reception — a statue with open arms in welcome. It is said that when he had to flee Rome into the vineyards, he was saved by a vine that suddenly grew around him and protected him.

There's much to admire in Schloss Zell from the pewter collection in the entrance hall to the variety of art treasures, tapestries vintners' tools and kitchen equipment. You can sleep in the room where Emperor Maximilian stayed in 1521 (No. 1), befittingly draped. Who can resist Tower Room No. 7's view of the vineyards? Who can resist Room No. 2, whose toilet is in the tower. Who can resist staying here at all?

The hotel is located in the centre of Zell, a town with gabled houses and a well-kept marketplace. It is within easy reach of Frankfurt and Koblenz.

5583 Zell/Mosel, Germany. ✆ (06542) 4084

7	(all with en suite bathroom)	✳	Intimately medieval
		🅿	No
🏨	Varies	♫	No
✕	Game and other German specialities	£/$	C

SPAIN

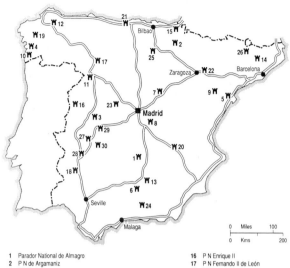

1. Parador National de Almagro
2. P N de Argamaniz
3. P N Carlos V
4. P N Casa del Baron
5. P N Castillo de la Zuda
6. P N Castillo de Santa Catalina
7. P N Castillo de Siguenza
8. P N de Chinchón
9. P N La Concordia
10. P N Conde de Gondomar
11. P N Condes de Alba y Aliste
12. P N Condes de Villalba
13. P N Condestable Dávalos
14. P N Duques de Cardona
15. P N El Emperador
16. P N Enrique II
17. P N Fernando II de León
18. P N Hernán Cortés
19. Hotel de los Reyes Catolicos
20. P N Marques de Villena
21. P N Gil Blas
22. Monasterio de Piedra
23. P N Raimundo de Borgona
24. P N San Francisco
25. P N de Santa Domingo de la Calzada
26. P N de Seo de Urgel
27. P N de Trujillo
28. P N Via de la Plata
29. P N Virrey Toledo
30. P N Zurbarán

One only has to look at Spanish history — with its counts, barons and kings — to realise there were countless castles, palaces and fortresses built over the centuries. Many still stand as places of touristic interest, splendid museum pieces. Others have been turned into hotels. Of the latter, the chain of paradores is perhaps the most exceptional.

The original idea was to establish affordable hotels in places of natural beauty, to encourage tourism. But another objective soon came into focus, that of restoring and refurbishing historical monuments in danger of disappearing. The Spanish government realised that converting buildings of artistic and historic value into paradores would not only enrich the traveller who stayed at them, but would preserve the country's own heritage. This is why today you can stay in a 12th-century castle like that at Benavente or a 14th-century palace like that in Alarcón.

Paradores offer value for money but are not necessarily luxurious. One chooses them for their uniqueness rather than health clubs and coffee shops. Generally they have one restaurant which serves regional cuisine, often as a set menu. The house, or jug, wine is usually surprisingly good. Don't expect colour TVs or mini bars in the rooms, nor swimming pools (only a few have them) — paradores are for atmosphere not amenities. And in the more out of the way places, a knowledge of Spanish can help. (I should point out that hosterias are also scattered throughout Spain. These, too, are sometimes converted historic properties but they are restaurants only, with no accommodation.)

Parador Nacional de Almagro

This pleasingly restored 16th-century convent is a useful overnight stop on the way to Granada or Málaga from Madrid. The Convent of San Francisco was built in 1596 by the Davila de la Cueva family and features 16 galleried patios. Its guest rooms are comfortable, if not luxurious; its air conditioning works as it should; and the staff are helpfully polite. Hotel conversion has given it a bodega (wine cellar) as well as bar and restaurant and an outdoor pool.

Many visitors are happy to stay here because the town of Almagro is so full of character. It is situated on the open plain of La Mancha, an important milestone on the don Quixote route and seat of the Order of the Knights of Calatrava.

The parador is 22 km (14 miles) from the city of Ciudad Real and 210 km (130 miles) from Madrid.

Ronda de San Francisco, Almagro, Ciudad Real, Spain.
✆ (926) 86 01 11

55	(mostly double, all with private bathroom)	✳	Warm and charming
		℘	Outdoor swimming pool
🏨	Year round	♫	No
✗	Regional dishes	£/$	B

Parador Nacional de Argomaniz

In the heart of Basque country, this hilltop parador used to be the Palace of Los Larrea. Don Juan de Larrea y Larrea studied at the University of Salamanca, was appointed Judge of the Grand Chancellery of Granada and was eventually made Minister of the High Council of Castile. It is a lovely peaceful country mansion, a good stopover for anyone entering or departing Spain via the French border at the western end of the Pyrenees.

Unlike other paradores, it boasts no garden but since it stands next to an uninhabited part of the village it may almost be considered to have a natural park. Food and furnishings are simple but the former is fresh and the latter, comfortable.

Argomaniz is situated 15 km (9 miles) from the provincial capital of Vitoria and 10 km (6 miles) from Mendoza.

Apartado 601 Vitoria, Argomaniz, Alava, Spain.
✆ **(945) 28 22 00**

48	(all double with en suite bathroom)	✳	Peaceful and simple
		℘	No
🏨	Year round	♫	No
✕	The speciality is snails and, when in season, los perros chicos (a type of mushroom)	£/$	C

Parador Nacional Carlos V

With a name like Carlos V you can be sure of the royal touch at this parador and yes, the Emperor with that name did stay here for almost three months in the 16th century.

The castle complex that is today's hotel was built towards the end of the 14th century on the orders of the Count of Oropesa and Marquis of Jarandilla. Made of local stone and graced by towers, its original fortified walls and drawbridge remain intact. A coat of arms of Carlos V can be seen on the main façade and many others decorate the central patio, notably that of the Alvarez de Toledo family. On one side of the front section of the patio is a cloister; on the other, large windows cut out of the stone. A large tree-shaded garden gives the parador an air of seclusion though it is an integral part of the village of Jarandilla de la Vera.

Located in the region of La Vera which extends to the slopes of the Sierra de Gredos mountains, the parador is 145 km (90 miles) from Ávila and 110 km (68 miles) from Guadalupe.

Jarandilla de la Vera, Cáceres, Spain. ✆ **(927) 56 01 17**

43	(mostly double)	✳	Noble and quiet
		℘	No
🏨	Year round	♫	No
✕	Typical of the region	£/$	B

Parador Nacional Casa Del Baron

Casa del Baron is a typical *pazo* or Galician manor house built on the site of a Roman villa. As its name suggests, it was a baron's home — the first owner was Don Benito de Lanzos, Grandee of Spain. It was handed down through the family and enlarged on several occasions until it became the property of the Marquis of Figueroa and La Atalaya. After his death in 1808, in the battle against the French at Rioseco, the beautiful house suffered the wear and tear of being a school, a public granary and a masonic lodge. Happily, it eventually came to belong to the Barons of Casa Goda whose last lord, Don Eduardo de Cea y Naharro, restored it magnificently. It was opened as a hotel in 1955.

The three star hotel is situated on the banks of the River Lerez in the centre of Pontevedra, a town that has several museums and monasteries worth visiting. There are beaches at Redondela, 20 km (12 miles) away and more *pazos* to be seen in Cambados, 24 km (15 miles) away.

Calle Maceda, Pontevedra, Spain. ✆ (986) 85 58 00

47	(mostly double)	✳	Countrified comfort
		℘	No
🏨	Year round	♫	No
✗	Regional specialities	£/$	B

Parador Nacional Castillo de la Zuda

La Zuda's hilltop location was once a prehistoric settlement, then a Roman acropolis and finally a Moorish fortress. Those with doubts about its history can still see the preserved well built in 944, in the times of Abd al-Rahman III, from which the parador takes its name. When the Count of Barcelona, Ramon Berenguer IV, reconquered Tortosa in 1178 he turned the castle into a royal residence though it also held the dual role of city prison. Later it was ceded to the Order of the Knights Templar.

Castillo de la Zuda is one of Spain's larger paradores with facilities that include a bar, children's play area and swimming pool. Public and guest areas are air conditioned and centrally heated, and the view from the dining room looks over the splendid fertile valley of the Ebro where fruit orchards, olive groves and rice fields can be seen. Four of the hotel's large windows and three of its fireplaces date from the 13th century, the time when a code of medieval laws were written — the most complete and advanced of its kind, now housed in the nearby Museo-Archivo Municipal.

Tortosa itself is an important touristic centre, noted for historic monument like the Convent of Santa Clara and the medieval commodity exchange of La Lonja. Its Gothic cathedral is one of the best examples of Catalan architecture and contains numerous works of art. Located 83 km (51½ miles) from Tarragona, whose architecture ranges from Roman to present times, the Castillo de la Zuda is a convenient base for hunting expeditions into the mountains and only some 28 km (17 miles) from the beaches of San Carlos de la Rapita and Alcanar.

Tortosa, Tarragona, Spain. ✆ (977) 44 44 50

82	(mostly double)	✻	Casual castle
🏨	Year round	⚲	Garden with children's playground, heated swimming pool
✕	Typical Catalonian with a variety of rice and fish dishes and including baby eel and frogs' legs	♫	No
		£/$	B

Parador Nacional Castillo de Santa Catalina

Although this is a new parador, the architect has shown so much respect for the original structure and the adjacent castle for which it is named, that the blend of old and new is most harmonious. The views from this eagle's nest are dizzying for the buildings of the parador are protected by inaccessible precipices (though there is a road to the city). South-facing balconied rooms are the best for stunning vistas.

Vaulted ceilings and priceless tapestries add the ancient touch; air conditioning and swimming pool, the new. Nearby Jaén still preserves its Moorish air and its cathedral is one of the best examples of Renaissance art in Spain.

Carretera del Castillo, Jaén, Spain. ✆ (953) 23 22 87

42	(mostly double, some balconied, all with en suite bathroom)	✳	New castle atmosphere
		℘	Swimming pool
🏠	Year round	♫	No
✕	Typical Andalusian dishes include la pipirrana (a cucumber and tomato salad) and a special spinach dish	£/$	C

Parador Nacional Castillo de Siguenza

If you are familiar with the multitudinous Spanish titles and personalities which ink the history books, you'll adore this four star parador, host to many and scene of files of events and altercations. Under the roofs of this castle-palace, Cardenals Mendoza and Cisneros spent time; so did the catholic monarchs, Juana la Loca, the Doncel de Siguenza, Fernando VII and his wife Maria Josefa Amalia and, far more recently, King Don Juan Carlos and his wife, Doña Sofia.

Originally, the structure was a Visigothic castle which in turn became a Moorish fortress and, after 1122, an episcopal stronghold. The Mendozas converted the castle into an episcopal palace and Juan Diaz de la Guerra, a descendant of Columbus, changed its interior to that of a civil palace. It was here at the end of the 13th century that the fight for the Crown of Castile took place between the Infante Alfonso de la Cerda and King Fernando IV. During the War of Spanish Succession, troops from both sides were housed here and during the War of Independence it was looted by Napoléon's troops then quartered in the palace.

During the earlier centuries, the western exit of the castle was used, called the Gate of El Campo, flanked by two small towers reconstructed by Bishop Don Simon Giron de Cisneros in the 14th century. Today's large dining room takes its name from the Tower of Doña Blanca on this side of the building. Later, the Bishop created another entrance, this time facing the city, also flanked by two towers — the gateway access used today.

Reconstruction and renovation to transform the palace into a hotel has been done sensitively enough to result in a pleasantly blended old/new combination. While the eastern wall had to be reshaped to allow for more light in the bedrooms and dining room, the Throne Hall and Romanesque chapel have scarcely been changed. To lighten the severe atmosphere of the paved inner court, a decorative elevated walkway with portcullis and small garden with 18th-century lamp posts have been added and the bar/café, kitchen and dining room are also new. But the fitments and furnishings are in keeping with traditional parador style — dark wood, effective ceramics, suits of armour.

Siguenza is situated on the left bank of the River Henares in a valley of orchards and pine trees, views of which are possible from some of the balconied bedrooms. Located 135 km (84 miles) from Madrid, the city is as full of monuments as those other cities within its vicinity like Guadalajara, noted for its Palace of the Duque del Infantado, and the Ducal City of Pastrana.

Siguenza, Guadalajara, Spain. ℒ (911) 39 01 00

82	(mostly double, most with bathroom)	✳	Glamorously medieval. Dramatic setting
🏨	Year round	♉	No
✕	Don't be too disappointed if the dining room setting is better than the food. Look out for specialities like roast kid and garlic soup	♬	No
		£/$	B

Parador Nacional de Chinchón

Chinchón's parador occupies a 17th-century Augustinian convent where friars taught diverse subjects, including Latin. When they lost their property under Mendizabal's Disentail Law, the State appropriated the building. It was later turned over to Chinchón by the Regent Luis Maria de Borbon to be used as a local courthouse and jail, a situation which continued until it was recently converted into a hotel.

Although the former convent still has a church within its confines and a slightly cloistered air, it is far cheerier than many other historic paradores, with bright and colourful Azueljo tiles and painted furniture. Guest rooms border a pretty courtyard garden with a central fountain and in the larger, landscaped back garden there's a swimming pool.

Avenida Generalisimo 1, Chinchón, Madrid, Spain.
✆ (91) 894 08 36

38	(all twin, all with en suite bathroom)	✳	Four star cheerfully relaxing
🏨	Year round	♪	Swimming pool and garden
✕	The local wine's cheap and the regional food good, such as Castilian soup, lamb and sausage	♫	No
		£/$	B

Parador Nacional La Concordia

Castle, convent, palace? This hotel is all three. Situated on top of a hill overlooking the town of Alcañiz, this was originally the seat of the Order of Calatrava to which it was given by Alfonso II in 1179. Today, the castle is a national monument whose best feature is its keep where Gothic wall paintings can be seen. There is also a small cloister with the sarcophagi of several masters of Calatrava. Juan de Lanuza, viceroy of Aragón built the bell tower-cum-vestry where he was host to Emperor Charles V.

Prince Felipe turned part of the castle into a palace in 1728 and it is this section which has become the hotel. The parador is easily accessible being located close to an important road junction. There are many interesting places that can be visited within a day, including Escatron and its Cistercian Monastery of Rueda.

Castillo de Calatravos, Alcañiz, Teruel, Spain.
✆ (974) 83 04 00

12	✳	Historic
	℘	No
🏨 Year round	♫	No
✕ Typical of Aragón, e.g.	£/$	B
pollo al chilindron (chicken		
with red pepper and tomatoes)		

Parador Nacional Conde de Gondomar

Above the sea, this parador is situated in a former fort and governor's palace, overlooking the Atlantic port into which the ship *Pinta* sailed in 1493 with the news of Columbus' discovery of the New World. On this site, Commander Viriatus defeated the Romans and established a stronghold. After the Moorish invasion, it was reconquered by Alfonso I in 750, only to be taken again by al-Mansur in 997.

The parador, situated in the grounds of this Monte Real fortress whose old walls and tower still remain, is modern enough to be a four star property, well run and comfortable.

Located on the coast, 18 km (11 miles) south of Vigo, the parador has been designed to resemble a typical Galician country manor. Beaches and a yacht club are nearby.

Carretera de Bayona, Bayona, Pontevedra, Spain.
✆ (986) 35 50 00

128	(mostly double, including suites; all with en suite bathroom)	✳	Modern comforts in old setting
🏠	Year round	℘	Swimming pool, tennis court, children's play area, sauna. Nearby beach, fishing and yacht club
✗	Seafood restaurant and Spanish tavern are among facilities		
		♫	No
		£/$	C

Parador Nacional Condes de Alba y Aliste

Zamora is one of those Spanish towns deeply involved with history — indeed, it was the stage for many events — and what better place to stay than at its heart in what was once the Palace of the Counts of Alba y Aliste. It was originally built by the first Count in 1459 but suffered severe damage during a 16th-century rebellion of the Communities of Castile, eventually put down by Carlos V. We have the fourth Count to thank for rebuilding and decorating it so magnificently. In 1798 it was extensively remodelled and converted into a hospice.

Now a hotel, the Renaissance cloister shows palatial splendour at its finest. Here, above the columns, medallions depict mythological and historical figures while another section is decorated with ancestral coats of arms. Look, too, at the beautifully preserved balcony and staircase enhanced by Lombardic carvings.

Though this parador is among Zamora's most noteworthy monuments, it is not without four star comforts like a bar and central heating, not to mention a delightful garden and swimming pool. Its location on the fringe of the oldest district inevitably eases sightseeing and there's plenty to see: the 12th-century cathedral with its Byzantine cupola and its museum; numerous churches like the 11th-century Church of Santiago de los Caballeros where it is said El Cid was knighted; old city walls.

Condes de Alba y Aliste sits on the right bank of the River Duero in the western foothills of the Castilian tableland, some 62 km (38½ miles) from Salamanca and 250 km (155 miles) from Madrid. A superb base we think for exploring and seeing many of Spain's medieval treasures.

Plaza de Canovas s/n, Zamora, Spain. ✆ (988) 51 44 97

27	(all double)	✳	Stately
		℘	Swimming pool, garden
🏨	Year round	♫	No
✕	Look for codfish 'tranca' style, and almond custard among the desserts	£/$	B

Parador Nacional Condes de Villalba

It is so peaceful in Villalba, a village overlooking the unspoilt flatlands of Galicia, it is difficult to think it was any other way. But today's parador was a fortress — one of the area's most important, the Tower of Los Andrade, a medieval bulwark of unknown origins.

As a hotel it is only small but its thick stone walls and high standard of furnishings more than compensate, and its octagonal tower reached via a drawbridge brings the medieval era to reality.

Situated 36 km (22 miles) from the provincial capital of Lugo, it could well be a pleasing stopover between Gijon and Santiago. Art lovers and history buffs will find plenty to interest them without having to travel too far. The town of Mondonedo (36 km, 22 miles away) is a history complex in itself with 12th-century cathedral, Monastery and Museum of Religious Art.

Valeriano Valdesuso s/n, Villalba (Lugo), Spain.
℡ (982) 51 00 11

6	(all double with bath)	✳	Cosy Spanish. Not suitable for children or the elderly
⌂	Year round	♪	No
✕	Expect to sample typical Galician cuisine	♫	No
		£/$	B

Parador Nacional Condestable Davalos

The building dates from the 16th and 17th centuries and was named for one of the city's most important personages in his day, though Condestable Davalos, held in high regard by Juan II, actually lived in the nearby House of the Towers.

The parador is in Greco-Roman style. At the main entrance the frieze shows a shield of Los Ortega held by several angels. Around it are most of the city landmarks: the Chapel of El Salvador, the Palace of El Marques de Mancera and the Palace of Vazquez de Molina. Ubeda is one of Spain's most traditional cities, once part of the Holy Realm, an historic gem in Sierra scenery, surroundings which will reward hunting and fishing fans.

It was opened as a hotel in 1929 but renovated in 1942 in more Renaissance style: The latter style deserves especial attention in Jaén, 57 km (35 miles) away. The Moors laid out the streets of Jaén and built the baths at Santa Teresa, their cultural aura still lingering today.

Plaza de Vazquez Molina s/n, Ubeda (Jaén), Spain.
✆ (953) 75 03 45

25	(24 double, 1 single)	✂	No, but the area is good for hunting and fishing
	Year round	♫	No
✕	Typically Andalusian	£/$	B
✳	Pleasantly unfussy		

Parador Nacional Duques de Cardona

On top of a conical hill that overlooks the River Cardoner is the castle parador of Duques de Cardona, a four star hostelry in a fortified complex whose focal point is the magnificent Romanesque complex whose focal point is the magnificent Romanesque church of San Vicente, and whose most remarkable feature is the 2nd-century tower called Minyona.

Woven cloth in jewel colours decorates corridors and guest rooms, and the arched and vaulted dining room has plenty of castle atmosphere in which to enjoy Catalan cuisine. It is a good base from which to go skiing at the nearby resort of Port del Comte (42 km, 26 miles) or to visit the provincial capital of Barcelona (97 km, 60 miles).

Cardona, Barcelona, Spain. ✆ (93) 869 12 75

65	(mostly double)	✱	Mod cons in ancient setting
🏨	Year round	⚓	Fishing is possible in the River Cardoner for trout, carp and pike
✕	Tasty fish stews, Catalan sausage, and sweet pastries like neulets		
		♫	No
		£/$	B

Parador Nacional el Emperador

This castle-cum-palace has seen innumerable royal guests. Perched above the border river with France in the centre of the seaside resort of Fuenterrabia, it was founded in the times of Sancho Abarca, King of Navarra, later enlarged by Sancho el Fuerto and fortified by the Catholic Monarchs.

Today's parador occupies both castle and palace areas, their ancient character evident in the massive stone walls and stairways, Gothic arches and slabbed stone courtyards.

Inside, there are beamed ceilings and polished wood floors. What is now the bar and lounge areas were the castle, while the guest rooms are the palace. The sea is only five minutes away and from the cove where the town lies, and the nearby mountain of Jaisquibel, you can see the River Bidasoa and France beyond. The disadvantage is that El Emperador no longer features a restaurant.

Fuenterrabia is located 21 km (13 miles) from the popular tourist centre of San Sebastian.

Plaza de Armas del Castillo, Fuenterrabia, Guipuzcoa, Spain. ✆ **(943) 64 21 40**

16	(mostly double; all with private bathroom)	✳	Old castle atmosphere
🏨	Year round	♪	No
✕	Breakfast only	£/$	B

Parador Nacional Enrique II

The exterior of the Enrique II looks rather grim and austere. It is, after all, a 14th-century castle-alcazar, a Moorish fortress with crenellated walls and a keep, that surveys the River Agueda from its hilltop site.

By way of contrast to its forboding appearance, the inside of the parador is cosily furnished in local Castilian fashion with lots of bright fabrics to cheer up the dark carved wood. From the beamed and arched dining room you can look out towards the river, the town of Ciudad Rodrigo and splendidly rural plains. And its own garden gives an added uplift.

This hotel is located on the edge of town, so seems secluded, but is in fact within walking distance of the centre. The walled city was built in the 12th century and has several notable monuments as well as viewing platforms.

Plaza del Castillo 1, Ciudad Rodrigo, Salamanca, Spain. ✆ (923) 46 01 50

28	(16 double, 12 single; all with en suite bathroom)	✳	Quite intimate and unshowy
🏨	Year round	℘	Fishing may be arranged in the nearby river
✕	Expect some Salamanca cuisine like el caderillo de Bejar	♫	No
		£/$	B

Parador Nacional Fernando II De León

Today's parador is the castle-cum-palace built in the times of King Fernando II of León for whom it was named and where parliament was assembled in 1176. The Renaissance building incorporates a particularly beautiful tower though I don't know why it has the name 'Tower of the Snail'. The Catholic Monarchs stayed at the castle on their pilgrimage to Santiago de Compostela, as did their children Doña Juana and Felipe el Hermoso; this century's guests will find more up-to-date four star comforts including air conditioning.

Fernando II De León is located on a hill just to the south of town, near the River Orbigo. It is some 65 km (40 miles) from Zamora and 69 km (43 miles) from León whose cathedral is the best example of 13th-century Gothic and has a unique collection of glass windows.

Benavente, Zamora, Spain. ✆ **(988) 63 03 00**

30	(mostly double)	✳	Quiet, elegant
		♪	No
🏨	Year round	♫	No
✕	Zamora cuisine tends to be spicy. Look out for el bacalao a la Tranca (a cod dish)	£/$	B

Parador Nacional Hernán Cortés

It has the imposing air of a castle but Parador Hernán Cortés was a fortified palace, not surprising when you realise that one-time tenant, Hernán Cortés, was to become the Conquistador of Mexico. He was a protégé of the Duke of Feria who owned the palace and lived here before departing for that 'New World'.

Work on the alcazar-turned-parador began in 1437 and was completed in 1443 under the direction of Don Lorenzo Suarez de Figueroa whose coat of arms, together with that of his wife, Maria Manuela, can still be seen on the building's façade and in parts of the interior. At the back of the square and towered edifice stands the keep; two towers protect the main gateway entrance.

Within, the most outstanding feature is the white marble Renaissance patio where columns of Doric and Ionic design support galleries — Juan de Herrera, who planned the Escorial, is accredited with its architecture. Master workmanship doesn't end there though for the chapel with its gold and dark blue Gothic cupola is equally impressive and the Golden Hall's ceiling is yet another work of art.

Zafra itself has that esteemed air of Andalusian elegance, so aristocratic it has been nicknamed 'Sevilla la Chica' (Little Seville). The Parador, though reconditioned to become a hotel by converting outbuildings to guest accommodation and adding a swimming pool, has lost none of its character or atmosphere.

Public rooms and guest areas are air conditioned and centrally heated, of course, but the cuisine served in the dining room remains typical of the Extremadura region. From the parador, which stands in flat ground within the town, it is easy to visit the Duke and Duchess of Feria's castle, the Convent of Santa Clara, the Plaza Grande and the Plaza Chica. There are many accessible places of interest from Zafra including Merida, 63 km (39 miles) away, Jerez de los Caballeros, 38 km (23½ miles) away (birthplace of Hernando de Soto and Vasco Nunez de Balboa).

Plaza de Maria Cristina s/n, Zafra, Spain.
✆ (924) 55 02 00

28	(mostly double; all with telephone)	✳	Retains the elegance and style of a past era
🏨	Year round	℘	Garden, swimming pool
✗	Typical regional food is usually served as is true of all paradors. Look out for caldereta de cordero (regional lamb dish) and pastorejo.	♫	No
		£/$	B

Hotel de Los Reyes Catolicos

This is probably one of the most historic and majestic of all the paradores, a memorable and monumental hotel in the centre of medieval Santiago. It was originally founded as a Royal Hospital in 1499 by Catholic monarchs, Ferdinand and Isabella, to give shelter and lodging to the pilgrims — so in a way it is one of the world's oldest hotels.

Built in the shape of an Etruscan cross, with four cloisters, it sits on one side of the wonderful square of the Obradoiro, the same square as the cathedral. Beautifully restored to become a five star hotel, its cloisters, Gothic patios, carved jambs were all given a great deal of respect during the work. Over 600 paintings decorate the rooms and galleries and the Royal Chapel has become an auditorium for concerts and exhibitions.

To stay here, most people agree, is an experience — an expensive one, but worth it. The guest rooms vary enormously, both in size and in furnishings, but many feature high ceilings, medieval Spanish furniture and canopied beds. An enormous vaulted crypt has become the main dining room though there is an elegant but more modestly priced cafeteria. Unique for a parador, not only for its amazing interior but for its facilities like shops and a discothèque.

Situated in the middle of town, it is 62 km (38½ miles)

from La Coruña.

Plaza de España 1, 15705 Santiago de Compostela, La Coruña Spain. ℘ (981) 58 22 00

|155| (including suites; all with en suite bathroom, colour TV, private safe)

🏨 Year round

✕ Specialities include octopus Galician style, hake in ajada and all types of traditional pies. Also almond cake made to a Santiago recipe.

✳ Synonymously medieval but plush

℘ No

♫ Discothèque nightclub. Concerts occasionally held in the Royal Chapel

£/$ A

Parador Nacional Marques de Villena

Marques de Villena is probably the best-preserved castle in the province of Cuenca. Named after the man who fortified it, today's parador looks as strong and noble as it did in the days when it was used for defence.

The surroundings are incomparable thanks to its majestic position on top of a huge rock almost completely encircled by the River Jucar. From the castle windows you can look over the town, the deep gorge and the river and the tilled plains of Cuenca.

This is only a small parador but an interesting one not too far from the provincial capital of Cuenca, famed for its 'hanging houses' which look so perilous as they jut from a sheer cliff. A few kilometres from Alarcón, the large artifical lake that forms Alarcón Reservoir provides the possibility for fishing and watersports.

Avenida Amigos del Castillo, Alarcón, Cuenca, Spain.
℡ (966) 33 13 50

11 (almost all double)		✳	Splendid preserved castle
		℘	Watersports at Alarcón Reservoir, 6 km (4 miles) away
Year round			
✗ Cuenca specialities			
		♫	No
		£/$	B

Parador Nacional Gil Blas

Gil Blas has to be one of the most popular and picturesque paradores in all Spain and particularly convenient for British visitors who have taken the ferry crossing to Santander, 31 km (19 miles) away. Until it recently added a new extension, doubling room availability, booking here was quite difficult.

The parador is actually an old and beautiful manor house once the county seat of the Barreda-Bracho family, that sits in a quiet cul-de-sac facing a cobbled square. Santillana itself is a showplace village of narrow cobbled streets, a working village that is surprisingly unspoilt, and one that is officially classified a national monument.

Gil Blas (named for the 18th-century-setting fictional character created by Le Sage) *feels* medieval though its creature comforts are decidedly 20th century. Guest rooms in the old section feature hand-made, highly polished, creaky oak floors and high oak-beamed and raftered ceilings, but the bathrooms are modern. You'll find the place attractive the moment you walk through the entrance door into a spacious hall with a pebblestone mosaic floor in the old style of the region.

Little more than 1½ km (1 mile) from the parador is The Prehistoric Museum and the famous Cuevas de Altamira. The prehistoric paintings date back to the 12th century BC and are located in caves which have been referred to as the 'Sistine Chapel of Primitive Art'. Santillana is 17 km (10½ miles) from the beach at Comillas and 63 km (39 miles) from the ski resort of Reinosa.

Plaza Ramon Pelayo 8, Santillana del Mar, Cantabria, Spain. ✆ (942) 81 80 00

57	(mostly double; all with en suite bathroom and TV)	✳	Delightfully atmospheric
🏛	Year round	♪	No
✕	Typical of Santander with plenty of fish dishes	♫	No
		£/$	B

Monasterio de Piedra

If you have never stayed in a monk's cell, the Monasterio de Piedra will give you the opportunity — in comfort. As you will gather, this hotel was formerly a 12th-century Cistercian monastery founded by order of Alfonso II of Aragón — and much of it is in a well-preserved state. In contrast to the stony countryside that surrounds it, the walled monastery complex is green, set in a park with waterfalls and lakes, medicinal springs and plane trees.

To explore the complex, visitors need only follow the direction of the red or blue arrows. Blue arrows lead from the Fuente de la Salud up to the Chorreaderos and the tunnel of the Cascada Iris (one of the lovely waterfalls). They direct you through the Valle del Vergel by the waterfall and grotto of La Carmela to Las Cuatro Calles and the Plaza Mayor. The grotto, discovered by Don Juan Federico Muntadas in 1860, put the natural finishing touch to his work on the site, and is best seen on a summer afternoon. Archaeological exploration begins at the Plaza: you will see the Patio del Surtidor, the Sala Capitular, the Gothic and Romanesque cloisters, the amazing 12th-century Tower of Homage, and the Fachada de la Antigua Hospederia.

Follow the red arrows from the Plaza de San Martin (in front of what is now the hotel) and you'll come to the Cuatro Calles which leads to the Mirador de la Cola de Caballo, another natural waterfall, 53 m (174 ft) high. Then on to the Cascada Iris and the Bano de Diana. From the Vergel, a rock-carved staircase reaches the Parque de Pradilla where a bridge crosses the river — a vantage point for admiring the Caprichosa waterfall. Returning to the Iris cascade, you descend past the Chorreaderos to the foot of the Cola del Caballo and trout farm. Then on to Mirror Lake and the Fuente de la Salud or spring of health whose medicinal waters are particularly recommended.

The hotel itself is as impressive as the grounds. As I mentioned, the monks' cells are today spacious bedrooms, all with en suite bathrooms and large tiled terraces. Hallways are wide with polished floors and the enormous lobby area has a superb Romanesque plastered ceiling with paintings and gilded rib vaulting. Service in the dining room, on Plaza de San Martin, is efficient and food of parador standards.

Monasterio de Piedra is located 28 km (17 miles) off the Zaragoza-Madrid road at Catalayud.

Nuevalos, Zaragoza, Spain. ⌀ **(976) 84 90 11**

61	(mostly double, including some suites; all with en suite bathroom and private terrace)	✳	Tranquil with beautiful outlook
🏨	Year round	℘	Outdoor swimming pool and tennis court in the gardens. Fishing and shooting nearby
✕	Standard parador-type fare		
		♫	No
		£/$	C

Parador Nacional Raimundo de Borgona

Once the Palace of Benavides (also known as Piedras Albas), this 15th-century parador makes up part of Avila's ramparts, reconstructed early this century.

Since it is situated within the city, it is central for seeing around Avila's multitudinous medieval monuments. Dating back to the 12th century, it was Europe's first fortified Romanesque city. The Royal Monastery of Santo Tomas here was the summer residence of the Catholic Monarchs — their son Prince Don Juan lies buried in its 15th-century Gothic sepulchre. Santa Teresa, one of the most important writers of the Spanish Golden Age, was born — and died — in Avila; many mementoes of her time are to be found in the museum of The Convent of San Jose, the first she founded.

Raimundo de Borgona stands on a ridge overlooking the River Adaja, 65 km (40 miles) from Segovia and 113 km (70 miles) from Madrid.

Marques de Canales y Chozas 16, Avila, Spain.
✆ (918) 21 13 40

62	(mostly double)	✳	Suited to sightseers
		✍	No
🏨	Year round	♫	No
✗	Regional specialities	£/$	B

Parador Nacional San Francisco

The position of this parador (within the Alhambra precinct near the Palace of Carlos V) necessitates its inclusion even though little remains of the Franciscan convent which originally stood here. Some people maintain it is one of the best paradores; others claim it is overpriced and serves food which is far from fantastic. All agree, though, that such memorable surroundings are worth any inadequacies and if you'd just removed yourself from the hot and tacky bar down the street — whose *vino tinto* was undrinkable — to its own elegantly serviced bar for highly palatable Rioja (as I did), you'd agree too.

The convent was built around a Mosque and Moorish palace constructed in the 14th century. Utilising the existing Moorish structures, the convent's High Chapel was built in the centre, surrounded by living quarters. This was the temporary resting place of Isabella and Fernando before their remains were transferred to Granada Cathedral's Royal Chapel in 1521. The site of that temporary sepulchre with commemorative plaque, the tower and the main entrance are the only portions to have been preserved, but modern architects have achieved an effective result with the rest of the hotel.

Since the parador is situated in its own garden within the Alhambra's walls, there is a unique view from the terrace across to the Generalife. El Albaicín can be also seen on the slopes of a nearby hill against a backdrop of the Sierra Nevada. Guest rooms are styled to recall the 18th-century monks' cells though they do have mod cons like bathrooms and air conditioning. Antique Spanish furniture fills the galleries and all the public rooms are decorated with pictures and engravings of the Spanish Romantic period. In the dining room locally crafted embroidery and wrought iron work is part of the décor.

The Alhambra itself is Granada's irresistible attraction, the world's only magnificently preserved, medieval Moorish palace. Only 35 km (22 miles) away the slopes of the Sierra Nevada are winter skiing territory. The holiday resort of Torremolinos is 143 km (89 miles).

Alhambra, Granada, Spain. ✆ (958) 22 14 93

34	(mostly double; all with private bathroom)	✳	Romantic and serene, thanks to memorable surroundings
▦	Year round		
✗	Reports on the food vary but look for typical Granada cuisine like the Trevelez ham and tortilla de Sacromonte (omelette)	℘	No
		♫	No
		£/$	B

Parador Nacional de Seo de Urgel

This parador is situated in the Romanesque quarter of El Urgellet's regional capital, Seo de Urgel — a survivor of the Middle Ages. Between the Cadi mountain range and the Andorra border, the town has been an episcopal seat for many centuries and its most important monument, the 12th-century Cathedral of Santa Maria, is not far from the hotel, itself a former church and convent.

These days, only the cloister remains preserved from the 14th century, forming an integral part of what has become a modern place to stay in the Lérida Pyrenees. Rated three star, the parador's facilities include an indoor heated pool, suite accommodation, air conditioning and central heating.

Something of a transit stop, Seo de Urgel is within easy reach of Andorra, 20 km (12 miles) away.

Seo de Urgel, Lérida, Spain. ✆ (973) 35 20 00

84	(60 double, 24 single)		charm but a good transit stop
🏨	Year round	℘	The forests and rivers of nearby Andorra are excellent for hunting and fishing
✗	Anticipate Catalan dishes like escudella (meat stew), botifarra and mongetes (white beans with sausage)		
✳	Lacks any real medieval	♫	No
		£/$	B

Parador Nacional de Trujillo

Trujillo's parador is fairly new (it opened in 1985) but it is located in an old 16th-century convent, founded by the Conceptionist Order. When Napoléon's troops arrived in 1809, the Clarisse Nuns had to move out and disperse and only a small number of them were able to return to their damaged cloister in 1811.

Though the convent has since been adapted to modern-day hotel standards, with a new annexe and tourist amenities such as air conditioning and central heating, a coffee shop and banqueting space, the older portion remains a simply designed building around a square cloister patio. Three sides of the granite cloister illustrate a Renaissance style with half-point arches resting on square pillars and Tuscan columns supporting an unadorned flat gallery above. Two beautiful granite staircases lead to the upper floor.

Modernity ensures that the plumbing works though guest room furnishings are a little austere, perhaps in keeping with a convent background. (For preference, opt for accommodation in the old section.) The parador is situated on a hill in the ancient citadel which was Pizarro's birthplace — his statue lords over Plaza Mayor, Trujillo's main square. The square, considered one of the finest in Spain, is flanked by many impressive buildings and arcades which can be viewed on foot.

Trujillo is located 47 km (29 miles) from the provincial capital of Cáceres, a walled National Monument enclosing towers and palaces. The pilgrimage centre of Guadalupe is 80 km (50 miles) away.

Plaza de Santa Clara, Trujillo (Cáceres), Spain.
✆ **(927) 32 13 50**

46	(all double, with 1 suite; most with bathroom)	✻	Modernised convent
🏨	Year round	🌱	No, though there is a garden
✕	Lamb stew and truffles are among the more typical dishes	♫	No
		£/$	B

Parador Nacional Via de la Plata

The whitewashed walls and monastery garden remind you that this parador was once a convent, built in fact over the site of a Roman temple.

Mérida is a popular tourist centre in western Spain with many superb Roman remains like the well-preserved theatre. It says something for the parador that it is highly patronised by the locals as well so that, while the rooms and corridors are quiet and tranquil, the bar and dining room may well be crowded and noisy.

Via de la Plata has been decorated simply but in keeping with the region with wrought iron and scattered wooden chests. Some of the bedrooms overlook the garden and terrace and the air conditioning is welcome relief in the height of summer. It has a reputation for friendly (if not terribly reliable) service and value-for-money food.

Plaza de Quiepo de Llano 3, Mérida, Badajoz, Spain.
℃ (924) 30 15 40

50	(mostly double; all with en suite bathroom)	✳	Frill-less, spotless and homely
🏨	Year round	℘	No
✗	Look for regional dishes like Andalusian lamb stew	♫	No
		£/$	B

Parador Nacional Virrey Toledo

Virrey Toledo is an imposing castle-cum-palace with a long, marked history and a commanding position on the slopes of the Sierra de la Ventorilla. From here there is a splendid view of the Campo Arazuelo and, in the background, the high Sierra de Gredos mountains. The site's fine position was the reason why it was chosen for the very first castle, back in 1716 BC, built by Hercules' soldiers who were on their way to Trujillo from Ávila in the company of Orospedus.

Virrey Toledo was converted into a parador in 1930. Hotel comforts like central heating have been added but the distinguished air has not been lost. Nearby Lagartera is famous for its embroidery and regional costumes; Talavera de la Reina (32 km, 20 miles away) is famous for its ceramics. Oropesa is located 150 km (93 miles) from Madrid.

Plaza del Palacio 1, Oropesa-Toledo, Spain.
✆ (925) 43 00 00

44	(mostly double)	✶	Super baronial
		℘	No
▦	Year round	♪	No
✕	The menu features fish and game	£/$	B

Parador Nacional Zurbarán

Zurbarán is a particularly charming parador that has the added asset of being within easy reach of the Monastery of Guadalupe whose famous 'Virgin' draws numerous visitors. Indeed, the place was originally the old Hospital of San Juan Bautista, established by the Monastery's prior, Fernando Yanez, to take care of the pilgrims who came to beg assistance from 'Our Lady'.

The Monastery is a treasure house of art: its museum not only houses a collection of 15th–18th-century miniatures but one of Europe's most valuable displays of embroideries and precious stones.

Guadalupe is 155 km (96 miles) from Toledo and 128 km (79½ miles) from Mérida.

Marques de la Romana 10, Guadalupe, Cáceres, Spain.
✆ (927) 36 70 75

20	(mostly double; most with bathroom, some with balcony)	✳	Pleasantly bright
		℘	Swimming pool in garden
🏨	Year round	♫	No
✗	Typical dishes include a rice soup and chestnut pudding	£/$	B

BRITAIN AND IRELAND

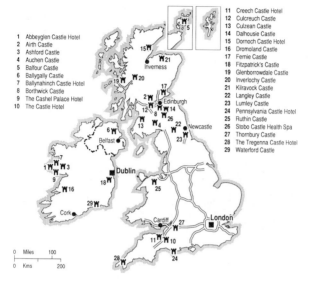

1 Abbeyglen Castle Hotel
2 Airth Castle
3 Ashford Castle
4 Auchen Castle
5 Balfour Castle
6 Ballygally Castle
7 Ballynahinch Castle Hotel
8 Borthwick Castle
9 The Cashel Palace Hotel
10 The Castle Hotel

11 Creech Castle Hotel
12 Culcreuch Castle
13 Culzean Castle
14 Dalhousie Castle
15 Dornoch Castle Hotel
16 Dromoland Castle
17 Fernie Castle
18 Fitzpatrick's Castle
19 Glenborrowdale Castle
20 Inverlochy Castle
21 Kilravock Castle
22 Langley Castle
23 Lumley Castle
24 Pennsylvania Castle Hotel
25 Ruthin Castle
26 Stobo Castle Health Spa
27 Thornbury Castle
28 The Tregenna Castle Hotel
29 Waterford Castle

If you want to find a castle hotel in Britain, head to Scotland where several baronial homes have been turned into hotels. Ireland, too, features some elegant and renowned ones, though England itself is a bit on the short side. (Most English castles have remained precisely that — museum pieces.) Some of the hotels which have been operating for years (e.g. Ashford Castle) have become widely known, but there has also been a recent flourish of transformations from privately owned historic properties to open-to-the-public hostelries.

Abbeyglen Castle Hotel

In all truth, Abbeyglen is not a genuine castle. (Indeed, those who may have visited Connemara in the past may have known it simply as the Abbeyglen Hotel.) But since 1970, under the energetic directorship of proprietor/manager Paul Hughes, they have been refurbishing, reconstructing and restoring. The original building (almost 200 years old) was an orphanage though you'll scarcely recognise what you see today from the old photographs.

As a hotel it has hosted numerous celebrities including the Rainiers, Peter O'Toole and Angela Lansbury, and its cuisine has been highly recommended by several notable foodies. Thanks to willing service and personalised proprietorship, Abbeyglen's guest welcome is a warm one. New décor and facilities have raised previous standards.

From Abbeyglen there's a panoramic view of Clifden and its bay against a backdrip of the 12 Bens mountain range. In its grounds is a heated outdoor pool, 9-hole mini golf course and a hard tennis court, and there are plenty of further sport possibilities in its vicinity. Fishing is particularly well catered for since Paul Hughes takes a personal interest, making bookings and arranging for packed lunches.

Although Abbeyglen is located on the Connemara coast, it is sheltered by its own 5 hectares (12 acres) of parkland valley. Galway is 80 km (50 miles) away, Knock, 121 km (75 miles) and Shannon, 177 km (110 miles).

Sky Road (near Clifden), Connemara, Co. Galway, Ireland ✆ (095) 21201

40 (all with en suite bathroom, colour TV and inhouse movies)

🏨 Year round, except for part of Jan

✕ Locally caught fish (including visitor's own) is a feature of the menu including salmon, lobster, prawns, mussels and scallops. Dishes are prepared French style

✳ Genial Irish atmosphere

♏ Heated pool and hard tennis court in the grounds. Facilities for table tennis and snooker (competition-sized table). Also a sauna and solarium and 9-hole mini golf. Nearest 18-hole golf course is a 24-km (15-mile) drive south at Ballyconneely. Riding may be arranged through local stables. Cleggan and Clifden have become centres for organised sea fishing; good salmon fishing waters are within easy reach as are trout lakes

♫ Resident pianist 6 nights a week, but spontaneous musical evenings are a frequent occurrence

£/$ C

Airth Castle

From a 13th-century baronial castle, Airth has become a superb four star hotel — one of the best for mod cons in a medieval manor. The name stems from the Gaelic 'Ardhe' signifying a hill and its situation is indeed a pleasant one overlooking the River Forth. A Grade A listed building, it has a host of historic features. Originally the fortified home of the Erth family, it passed by marriage to the Bruce family in the 15th century and to the Elphinstons in the 16th.

The earliest part of the castle, the west wing, was a simple stone tower which was later incorporated into a much larger, more comfortable residence designed in a Z shape, characteristic of the 16th and 17th centuries. The windows of the south front were enlarged in 1690 and the north front (now the main entrance) was added in 1803.

This is the place for those who like elegance without too much formality, professional standards of service and facilities. Public rooms are spacious with good views of the surrounding countryside, and include a dining room, cocktail bar, comfortable lounge and a converted dungeon that may be used for private parties. Bedrooms are individually decorated — those in the corner towers actually have circular bathrooms!

Close to the castle itself and reached via the cobbled courtyard is a converted stable block built of local stone. This has become Airth's conference centre and country club complex which houses additional guest rooms, its own cocktail bar and the Stables restaurant which stays open all day to 10 pm. Within the leisure centre is an octagonal-shaped pool area complete with jacuzzi, sauna, gym, sun beds and a billiard room. So I wasn't kidding about facilities. And there's 5 hectares (12 acres) of woodland in which to work or relax peacefully.

Situated on the edge of Scotland's central belt with easy motorway accessibility from Edinburgh and Glasgow, Airth is an excellent touring base. The beautiful scenery for which Scotland is renowned is literally all around it: the Ochil Hills to the north, the Trossachs and Loch Lomond to the west, fishing villages and the links of Fife to the east.

Airth, by Falkirk, Stirlingshire, Scotland.
℗ (032 483) 411

46	(7 single, 15 double, 24 twin, some four posters; all with en suite bathroom and TV with in-house movie channel. Rates include full Scottish breakfast)	✳	Modernity with a difference
		℘	Golf, fishing and shooting can be arranged through the hotel
🏰	Year round	♫	No
✗	First class food and wines	£/$	B

Ashford Castle

A fairy-tale setting on the shores of Lough Corrib makes this hotel almost incomparable among Europe's premier castle hotels, and its history is worth the booking of even its more modern rooms.

Within its castellated façade, for instance, are indeed the remains of a 13th-century de Burgo castle. No visitor can miss the exquisite examples of medieval craftmanship, most notably in The Great Hall where a 14th-century, Dutch-carved oak table holds a central position as a priceless antique. It is thought that such treasures were imported by Spanish traders doing business through the Port of Galway in the 1300s.

Ashford is renowned for its meticulously carved wood-work, such as the unique oak inglenook and fireplace which reaches over 6 m (20 ft) to the ceiling in the Reception Room. The adjoining Corrib Lounge is also worth considerable attention, particularly for its carved oak, ebony-inlaid fireplace where you can see the figurehead of King Roderick O'Connor, the last native to hold the title of High King of All-Ireland.

Later in its history, during Charles II's reign, a French-styled château was incorporated into the castle. Parts of this remain visible in the present main entrance and some of the guest rooms. The roof turreting, on the other hand, was carried out under the supervision of Sir Benjamin Lee Guinness when he bought the property in 1852 and his son,

Lord Ardilaun, was instrumental in vast improvements to both house and estate. He generated electricity here when few places in Ireland had such a luxury and brought in his own special train on the Midland Railway's Dublin run. He developed shooting on the estate and Ashford became famous in Europe for woodcock. What's more, the magnificence of the grounds today is largely due to his foresight.

Transformation from mansion home to luxury hotel began in 1939 when the then owner, Noel Huggard, can be thanked for establishing Ashford as *the* elegant place to stay in Ireland. He kept the castle self-sufficient during the war years by maintaining his own farm, dairy, slaughter house, modern butchery department, fishery and salmon smoking plant.

Ever since, the hotel's guest book has been filled with celebrity names, John Wayne among them when *The Quiet Man* was filmed here. Today's guests can enjoy sitting in the Oak and River Lounges where the Prince of Wales was entertained in 1908, though they also have modern amenities like en suite bathrooms and colour TVs. They dine on haute cuisine and latenight revel in the dungeon bar.

Ashford feels spacious — and it is, with what seems like panelled lounge after panelled lounge and grounds so extensive you won't even realise when the hotel is fully occupied. There are walkways, tennis courts and a small private golf course. In season, driven pheasant, duck and rough shooting are possible on the 10,935 hectares (27,000 acres) of preserves over which the castle has shooting rights. Lake Corrib itself offers great fishing waters for salmon and trout, or is equally attractive for a day's boating with hotel-packed lunch.

Located 48 km (30 miles) from Galway City, Ashford may easily be used as a base for exploring the scenic West of Ireland's fabled Connemara country.

Cong, Co. Mayo, Ireland. ✆ (094) 71444

84 (including some suites; all with en suite bathroom)	✳ Excellent — priceless décor, historic setting, vast grounds and magnificent views
▥ Apr–Dec	
✗ Though dishes sound exotic enough, quantities can be small and service sometimes under par. Nevertheless, Ashford has an international reputation and many culinary awards to its credit. Choice of two restaurants but note last orders, 9.30 pm	℘ Superb — notably shooting and fishing, 9-hole golf course, tennis
	♫ In the Dungeon Bar. Piano music with dinner
	£/$ A

Auchen Castle

Auchen Castle stands as an imposing sandstone mansion in Robert Burns and Sir Walter Scott countryside. Its origins are thought to date back to Sir Humphrey de Kirkpatrick in the 13th century when he was Seneschal of Annandale. Built in the form of a courtyard castle, its solid drum towers flanking the gate and corner tower were rebuilt, around 1304, as hollow turrets with internal stairs. The original castle has massive outer ramparts but its underground passage and chamber, it has been found out, were built in the early 19th century when a wooden chalet with eight chimneys stood above the passage as the place where guests were entertained after shoots.

Where you'll stay today, 3 km (2 miles) north of the actual castle, was constructed as a private house in 1849 — the home of Sir William Younger and his family for some 100 years. You won't find ornate drapery and priceless antiques here, though there is a worn grandeur, and friendly service. I note that adjectives like 'modest' are used to describe furnishings and 'compact', the bathrooms but I do know that the present resident owner Robert Beckh has made a number of improvements to both guest rooms and kitchen.

Today's Auchen hotel may be less historic than others mentioned in this book, but it is a comfortable value-for-money overnight stop with a commanding position overlooking Upper Annandale. Everyone agrees its gardens are superb — 20 hectares (50 acres) worth of grounds planted with specimen trees and shrubs and particularly colourful in spring with flowers. It has its own trout loch plus fishing rights to use the River Annan... other sport facilities are with easy reach.

Probably greatest praise goes to its food, not French-frills style, but delicious and copious enough to earn it a 'Taste of Scotland' commendation. (The restaurant features Saturday night dinner dances between March and October.)

Located 1½ km (1 mile) north of Beattock Village — access is signposted from the A74 — on a hillside with views over Upper Annandale, Auchen lies some 88½ km (55 miles) from Edinburgh and Glasgow, 66 km (41 miles from Carlisle. Not only a useful overnight stop it offers discounted family and sporting breaks.

Beattock, Moffat, Dumfriesshire, Scotland DG10 9SH.
✆ Beattock (068 33) 407

25	(13 twin and double, 2 single in the main house, 10 twin and double in the modern Cedar Lodge annexe; all with en suite bath or shower, colour TV and complimentary tea/coffee trays)	✳	Pleasant rather than special, well suited to families
🏨	Year round, except Christmas and New Year	℘	Reasonable. A trout loch with boat on the grounds; fishing rights on 5 km (3 miles) of the Annan River; golf at Moffat and Dumfries; tennis at Moffat; riding at Beattock and Dumfries. Rough shooting, sailing and hill walking is also possible in the vicinity
✗	Arbroath Smokies for breakfast, Galloway beef, Border lamb, Solway salmon and trout for dinner followed by creamy puddings. Fixed priced meals are generously portioned; excellent value	♫	Saturday dinner dance from Mar–Oct
		£/$	C

Balfour Castle

Balfour Castle is not a hotel in the accepted use of the word — it is still a private home. But it has opened its doors to a limited number of guests, travellers adventurous enough to discover the charm of the Orkneys.

Scotland's great Victorian architect, David Bryce, designed this splendid baronial home built in 1847 for Colonel David Balfour, at the time the most important resident landowner in Orkney. Indeed it was Balfour who created the chessboard-pattern fields that today the towers and battlements overlook. He claimed he was a descendant of the 11th-century Duncan — certainly his ancestors were Fife-shire barons — which is perhaps why he wanted his home to have a pseudo-feudal façade, an image of ancient lordship.

Of the 200 or so buildings which David Bryce designed or refashioned in Scotland, five were in Orkney and Balfour Castle is considered the finest example of his early work. Its style is typical: a square castellated tower with corner turret, the Pinkie bartizans and bay windows, an irregular exterior masking a comfortable and symmetrical interior. You'll note that the oak-panelled library and dining room are characteristic of the Victorian era.

The history and legends that surround the Balfours are numerous. It was only with luck that, after the last laird's death in 1961, Orkney's librarian accepted 50,000 documents from the castle and later persuaded the County Council to house them, making them and other Orkney records available to scholars and researchers. Today, the Balfour papers are the finest family collection in the Orkney Archives.

It was Capt. Tadeusz Zawadzki, a Polish Lancer who settled in Britain after the war, who saved the castle from neglect when he purchased it along with the farm of Balfour Mains. He and his Scottish wife are your hosts today.

The beautifully green island of Shapinsay is a 25 minute ferry trip away from Kirkwall. If offers visitors several easily accessible sandy beaches, many interesting walks, dramatic shorelines and abundant birdlife. The privately owned MV *Swilkie* may be chartered for closer viewing of seabird colonies, the skipper himself a keen ornithologist. Shapinsay is also the most intensely cultivated of the Orkney islands, exporting quality beef and sheep each to Aberdeenshire farmers for further fattening. Traditional Orkney crafts: boat building, knitting and wood carving are all carried on here, too.

Orkney is best reached by air from other parts of the UK. Flights arrive at Kirkwall, the capital town.

Shapinsay, Orkney Isles, Scotland ✆ (0856 71) 282

☐	Space for 6 guests in what is still a private home	✳	Away from it all retreat
🏛	Check	℘	The area is good for birdwatchers
✕	Fresh produce. Rates include full board plus wine with evening meal	♫	No
		£/$	A (but full board)

Ballygally Castle

Ballygally Castle may be located in Northern Ireland, but it was built by a Scot in 1625. James Shaw (a native of Greenock in Scotland with ancestry back to MacDuff, Thane of Fife in AD 834) came to this area in 1613 and built a home for himself and his wife, Isabella Brisbane. Their initials and family coats of arms are still inscribed over what was the main entrance leading to the tower.

Designed to French château style with high walls, steep roof, dormer windows and corner turrets, the castle was built of local stone. The 1½-m (5-ft) thick walls have withstood the test of time and some of the original carvings above the windows are still traceable.

The Shaw family managed to survive both rebellion and attack: in 1641 when the castle was used for shelter, the Irish garrison stationed at Glenarm failed to gain entry and, even when plundered in 1680, it remained a family stronghold. Additions were made around the middle of the 18th century when Henry Shaw, then squire, not only married but invited his two sisters-in-law to come and live in the castle.

Why only one of those sisters was said to have haunted the property for many years, no one knows, but it is alleged she (Madame Nixon) was seen on countless occasions in this century, walking the passages at night dressed in silk, knocking on various doors for her own amusement.

Ballygally was passed down from fathers to sons until the last squire, William Shaw, in 1799, who sold the estate to

Jones Agnew for £15,400. When the lease expired it was occupied as a coastguard station for a time until the Rev. Classon Porter and family took up residence. Much later it was owned by the Moore family who eventually sold it in the early 1950s to Cyril Lord and it became a hotel.

Nowadays there is a modern extension of guest and public rooms, not very in keeping in looks with the fine old castle structure. Be consoled that extension and renovation has resulted in the comforts of en suite bathrooms and central heating, and the dungeon cocktail bar in the cellars of the old fortress does at least maintain some of that historic atmosphere.

Indeed, in many ways this is a traditional hotel, providing a full Irish breakfast for its overnight room rate and continuing to feature a Saturday night dinner dance.

The hotel is located on the North Antrim coast, 40 km (25 miles) from Belfast, 8 km (5 miles) from Larne Harbour (terminus of the sea route from Scotland), its front facing the golden sands of Ballygally Bay, so the view is magnificent. There is a trout stream on its own grounds and an 18-hole golf course 1½ km (1 mile) away. It is ideally situated for visiting the famous nine glens of Antrim, taking scenic walks and finding local cottage industries.

Ballygally, Co. Antrim, N. Ireland. ✆ Ballygally 83212/4

29	(1 suite, individually if not excitingly decorated; all with private bathroom, colour TV and complimentary tea/coffee tray)	✳	Comfortably informal, suited to families. Historic links a plus factor
		♐	Fishing on grounds. 18-hole golf course 1½ km (1 mile) away
🏬	Year round	♫	No
✕	Typical Irish fare and international à la carte menu (table d'hôte lunch only). Candle-light dinner dance every Sat	£/$	C

Ballynahinch Castle Hotel

The name means 'household of the island' — the castle that the O'Flaherty clan, one of Ireland's most powerful families, built. Perhaps its most famous resident was Grace O'Malley, the pirate queen of Connaught, who married Donal O'Flaherty in 1546, when only a slip of a girl of 16. Herself from a powerful family, she was one who stood no nonsense — the history books relate of her piratical exploits and her 1593 meeting with Queen Elizabeth I — and after her husband's death she provided a formidable head of the family. A portrait of her still hangs over the fireplace in the bar, painted by the American artist Cleeve Miller.

Although Grace's son Murrough kept possession of the castle until the early 17th century, the O'Flaherty estate was sold to the Martin family in 1590, a family whose ancestry goes back to the Fourteen Tribes of Galway. When Richard Martin, 'Humanity Dick', was born in 1754, the family home was at Dangan, whilst the present house at Ballynahinch built by his father was used as an inn. But after it was renovated in 1813, 'Humanity Dick' moved there permanently.

Richard Martin, like his good friend the Prince Regent, later to become King George IV, was a colourful character noted for his lavish hospitality along with his duelling skills. He was also MP for the area and is most remembered for his

1822 bill introduced to the House of Commons as the 'Cruelty to Animals Act'. It was the passing of this bill that gave rise to the Society for the Prevention of Cruelty to Animals, and thus his nickname.

During the early part of the 19th century, Ballynahinch hosted many famous people: authoress Maria Edgeworth was to remark of the food 'it is worthy of the greatest gourmet', while Thackeray extolled the fishing opportunities. The Irish Famine, however, left the Martin's estate heavily encumbered and eventually it had to be sold to the Berridge family. The estate's superb fisheries didn't go unnoticed though. The Maharaja Jam Sahib of Nawanagar (Ranji, the cricketing prince) enjoyed the sport and Connemara's rugged scenery so much, he purchased the property in 1924. Thanks to his wealth the gardens and woods were landscaped and fishing piers and huts erected along the river. He arrived every summer to enjoy his buy, with several limousines in tow which he would later donate to the local residents before his return to India.

After Ranji's death in 1932 his nephew sold the castle to the McCormack family from Dublin and in 1946 the Irish Tourist Board took over the reins, running Ballynahinch as a hotel which continued to attract the notable: writer Liam O'Flaherty was a regular visitor, Sir Alec Guinness another guest. It has passed back in to private hands several times since, including Edward Ball, an American businessman whose business successor, Raymond Mason, has made vast improvements and welcomed past US President, Gerald Ford, across his threshold in 1981.

The castle, more comfortable than stately, overlooks the Ballynahinch River in the heart of Connemara, on a 142-hectare (350-acre) estate that offers kilometres of scenic walks. Located 66 km (41 miles) from Galway City and 40 km (25 miles) from Rossaveal, it is possible to visit the Aran Islands. The immediate area's own craft shops give excellent value in tweeds.

Ballinafad, Connemara, Co. Galway, Ireland
✆ (095) 31006

20	(individually named and decorated; all with en suite bathroom)	✳	Sporty orientated
		℘	In a good area for fishing and shooting — arrangements can be made. Tennis, driving range, nearby pony treks
▥	Year round		
✕	Local fresh produce		
		♫	No
		£/$	B

Borthwick Castle

Twin-towered baronial Borthwick Castle was built as a stronghold in 1430, designed in an E shape with 30-m (100-ft) walls, 6 m (20 ft) at the base. The early Borthwicks were all warriors — story has it that they encouraged their prisoners to jump the 3½-m (12-ft) gap between the towers, hands tied behind them. Those who achieved the jump were granted their freedom.

But the lords also entertained at many a banquet in the Great Hall, even today one of Scotland's most magnificent and the place where 20th-century guests dine by candle-light under its 12-m (40-ft) Gothic arch. To the right of the great hooded fireplace there is a seat of honour with carved canopy and shield bearing the Borthwick arms. Skilled stone masons created the four spiral staircases within the Great Hall's wall, leading to the Minstrel's Gallery, the bedrooms and battlements above and the dungeons below.

The most romantic association with the castle is Mary Queen of Scots who, together with her husband, sought refuge here in 1567. She had enjoyed the hospitality of the sixth Lord of Borthwick may times but on this occasion the castle was a sanctuary. The State Room, where she danced with the Earl of Bothwell, and the small chapel where she prayed are today the guests' drawing room, while the bedrooms they used are favourites, featuring four poster beds.

Had the Queen stayed under the protection of the

Borthwicks perhaps history would have been different. As it was, on 11 June in 1567 Lord Home surrounded the castle and Bothwell escaped leaving Mary behind. Even though (to show good intentions) Home's forces began to withdraw, Mary disguised herself as a page boy, climbed through a window of the Great Hall and went in search of her husband. She was never to know real freedom again.

Nearly a century later Borthwick's loyalty was again put to the test when Cromwell besieged it in 1650. The castle still bears the scars caused by Cromwell's cannon, though the ninth Lord Borthwick was compelled eventually to surrender rather than see its complete destruction.

Though 20th-century amenities like central heating and bathrooms have been introduced, this stately home remains very much a medieval masterpiece. Set in 8 hectares (20 acres) of grounds girded by a trout stream, the hotel has access to a further 18,225 hectares (45,000 acres) on which fishing and shooting can be arranged.

Located on the edge of Sir Walter Scott's Border country some 19 km (12 miles) from Edinburgh, Borthwick is signposted at the village of North Middleton.

North Middleton, Gorebridge, Midlothian, Scotland EH23 4QY. ✆ **(0875) 20514**

10	(5 double, 5 twin; all with period décor and en suite shower and toilet)	✳	Historically romantic
		℘	Shooting, fishing, riding and golf may all be arranged locally
⌂	Mar–Dec		
✗	Scottish food at its best including fresh salmon, Aberdeen Angus beef, Scotch lamb and game in season	♫	No
		£/$	B

The Cashel Palace Hotel

Saint Patrick first took up a shamrock while preaching to the people at Cashel, inadvertently providing Ireland with its most famous emblem. This ancient town dominated by its Rock was the seat of the Kings of Munster for seven centuries. The Cashel Palace on the other hand doesn't date that far back, but instead, an elegant Palladian mansion built in 1730 by Bishop Bolton which was to serve as a Bishop's Palace for 230 years.

Today it is owned and run as a luxury hotel by Ray Carroll, but even in 1732 it was described by Loveday as 'a place of notable hospitality'. Guests such as Dean Swift were invited then to see King Cormac's Chapel and possibly partake of a 'toast or two'. Archbishop Bolton's wine cellars still exist with the original painted numbers on the bins, and the dark stout produced here some 25 years later, under the patronage of Archbishop Arthur Price, eventually became world famous.

Architected by Sir Edward Lovett Pearce with a Queen Anne-style red brick façade, Cashel Palace is undoubtedly a handsome building. If you look above the entrance on the northern stone-faced side you'll see a fire mark issued by the Hibernian Insurance Company in the 1770s, showing a crowned harp. Inside, the main feature is red pine panelling — in the entrance hall, but more particularly on the great staircase where it reaches to a high ceiling.

After the Church Temporalities Act of 1833 when the last Archbishop, Richard Laurence, moved to Waterford, Cashel suffered ugly partitioning which has since been removed. Today, guest rooms are far more comfortable and prettier than any archbishop would have known them though many on the second floor still boast original fireplaces. Today, a stylish dining room overlooks garden greenery and a cellar bar has become a popular rendezvous, but the house displays many beautiful pictures and the 'Queen Anne' mulberry on the lawn is said to have been planted in 1702.

Cashel's gardens stretch from the back of the house to the slopes of the Rock which is framed by the same copper beeches which so delighted H.D. Inglis when he wrote about them in his book *Ireland in 1834*. Exclusive for guest use is the 'Bishop's Walk', a pathway which winds its way from the hotel to the Rock.

Though there are no on-site sport facilities there are plenty nearby: Tipperary is home of the Irish bloodstock industry with a number of famous stud farms and riding schools close to Cashel plus the Curragh racecourse. The region is also noted for shooting and fishing. Located at it is, almost equidistant from Limerick and Rosslare, the palace is an ideal touring base.

Cashel, Co. Tipperary, Ireland. ✆ Cashel 61411

20	(3 suites, 15 double, 2 single; all with private bathroom, colour TV and individual décor)	✳	Renewed elegance, quiet and courteous service
🏨	Year round	℘	No, but 3 golf courses, fishing, riding nearby
✕	Fresh produce is used as much as possible in the star-rated Four Seasons Restaurant. The Bishop's Buttery is for informal dining (both table d'hôte and à la carte)	♬	No
		£/$	B

The Castle Hotel

On the outside this is a splendid castle; on the inside it is a luxurious country house hotel. This site was once part of a Norman fortress, residence of the Bishops of Winchester whose ownership is commemorated by the painted Arms of the See of Winchester that you see today high up on one of the hotel walls. Over the years it has been razed by the Danes, besieged by Henry VII and captured during the Civil War. In 1685 Monmouth's officers were heard 'roystering at the Castle Inn' before his defeat at Sedgemoor — only a few months later Judge Jeffreys held the Bloody Assize in the castle's Great Hall.

When the castle itself was dismantled, part of it became a hostel so guests have continued being welcomed here for the past 300 years. Just as today, with its reputation for pampering its guests, in the 18th and 19th centuries the hotel provided quite elaborate facilities for travellers on the King's highway both in accommodation and post chaises. Not only were the proprietors ready with post chaises at a moment's notice, but the Bath coach and the Exeter coach left the hotel every day.

Royalty, past and present, have been visitors: Queen Victoria and her mother, King Edward VII and King Edward VIII when he was Prince of Wales and, more recently, the Queen Mother, Queen Elizabeth and Princess Margaret. Politicians, too, have been patrons; Disraeli addressed the electors of Taunton from the portico of the hotel after his electoral defeat in 1835.

If you're interested in history, look at the archway under the south wing of the hotel — it was originally the Eastern Gate or Porter's Lodge, built around 1300 and restored in 1495 by Bishop Langton. The grooves in which the portcullis was raised and lowered are still visible. The walls of one side of the present entrance hall also date to 1300 — you can see the ancient brickwork through a glass picture panel. As for the shields around the frieze of the entrance hall, they're genuine fire marks issued by early fire insurance companies.

Traces of the fortress can be seen in the moated garden including a wall of what was the inner moat, built in 1160, and a square Norman well, one of two existing in England today.

As you might expect, The Castle displays its fair share of antiques inside like the old tapestries hung in the panelled Oak Room, but the décor is by no means medieval but rather pastel chintz. Bedrooms are a delight, all individually furnished on a theme — mahogany, walnut, yew, painted bamboo.

The Castle's cuisine has won it many a star and rosette even with a change in chefs and the hotel prides itself on its wine list. British food critic Craig Brown claims its choice of clarets and burgundies 'is amazing'.

Taunton is a two hour rail journey from London and is accessible via the M4 and M5. At the heart of some of England's most beautiful and historic countryside, the hotel is a good base from which to explore the West Country.

Castle Green, Taunton, Somerset, England TA1 1NF.
✆ (0823) 272671

38	(11 single, 23 double and twin, 4 suites; all with en suite bathroom, colour TV)	✳	Prestigious country house appeal
🏨	Year round	℘	No, but arrangements can easily be made for golf, tennis, swimming and shooting
✕	Award winning, plus cellar with 300 wines		
		♫	No, except on special weekends
		£/$	B

Creech Castle Hotel

Ivy-clad Creech Castle Hotel is the incredible mansion Captain George Beadon had built in 1849 to house his large family when he retired from the navy. In 1840 he had taken part in the first Chinese war to protect the English opium trade which led to the creation of Hong Kong as a Crown colony. When he returned in Britain in 1841 he had a major portion of the $6 million Chinese ransom paid to regain Canton — more than enough to pay for the mansion's construction plus land to form a 60-hectare (150-acre) estate around it.

Although this castle hotel lacks the ancient stones and atmosphere of some, it does offer value for money for those wishing to explore the Somerset area. Its restaurant indeed is popular with the locals for traditional Sunday lunch and its easy access from the M5 plus ample parking space sites it conveniently for touring.

Bathpool, Taunton, Somerset, England TA1 2DX.
✆ (0823) 73512

28	(single and family, all with private bathroom, colour TV and tea/coffee trays)	✳	Family style
		℘	Not on site
		♫	No
▥	Year round	£/$	C
✕	À la carte menu		

Culcreuch Castle

Until recently, Culcreuch Castle was owned and lived in by the Baron and Baroness of Culcreuch — an ancestral home since 1699. But its history goes back to 1320 when it was seat of one of the principal branches of the Galbraith clan for 300 years, occupying a strategic position above the Endrick Water at the gateway to the hills. Records certainly show a Maurice Galbraith dwelt here in 1320 and the experts reckon the barrel-vaulted cellars, the spiral staircase and the bottle dungeon (so called for its shape — prisoners were unable to lie down) date from that period. The medieval tower, with walls over 1½m (5½ ft) in places, was completed by James Galbraith in 1460, topped by a parapet; later, a Georgian wing was added on to the east side rising to the same height as the tower.

There is much to see from all periods of its past, one of the reasons no doubt The National Trust for Scotland has described Culcreuch as a 'gem of outstanding beauty'. The Carved Hall, for example, is part of the 1721 extension and contains a wonderful assortment of carved furniture. It leads to the brass handrailed main staircase, a Georgian spiral one of braided stone.

The handsome mahogany table in the dining room dates back to William IV, as does the panelling. In the passage outside, a host of family portraits grace the walls, including that of Sir Hercules Robinson, an admiral who fought at Trafalgar as a midshipman.

Several pieces of typical Victoriana are to be seen in The Picture Drawing Room including a tapestry firescreen, inlaid piano and beaded picture of Culcreuch. The 100-year-old silvered wallpaper is irreplaceable. So is the hand-painted Chinese wallpaper, imported in 1723, which covers the Castle's most unique room — The Chinese Bird Room. It is said to be haunted by 'an amiable ghost' — a Galbraith was certainly murdered in this very room in 1582.

Perhaps the most imposing room (often now used for banquets) is The Laird's Chamber comprising the whole of the first floor of the 1460 keep. Its unusual frieze around the ceiling is protected by the Historic Monuments Association and equally unusual is its aumbry (a decorated wall recess) normally only found in ancient monasteries.

All meals are taken in the castle though the majority of the accommodation is in Scandinavian-style chalets set adjacent. The view is breathtaking: lawns run down to a 2-hectare (5-acre) loch and beyond is the tiny village of Fintry. The surrounding area is one of the most unspoilt in Scotland yet Glasgow is only 30½ km (19 miles) away and Edinburgh little more than an hour's drive.

Fintry, Stirlingshire, Scotland G63 0LW.
✆ (036 086) 228

6	(double and twin, all with en suite facilities) plus 8, 3-bedroom chalets adjacent	✳	A great deal of history in idyllic rural setting
🏠	Year round	🌳	The 648 hectares (1600 acres) of park and woodland provide the opportunity for rough shooting and a multitude of walks. Two lochs and the Endrick River may be fished
✕	Traditional Scottish breakfasts and baronial banquets are key features. Exceptionally reasonably priced five course table d'hôte dinners		
		♫	Only for groups
		£/$	C

Culzean Castle

So far as this book is concerned, Culzean Castle is somewhat unusual and terribly exclusive. It is not a hotel, but thanks to The National Trust for Scotland, a guest flat has been made available for business use or private individuals' hospitality.

The castle is a superb example of Robert Adam workmanship. Dating from 1777, it was designed by him for David, 10th Earl of Cassillis and took 15 years to build. Of exceptional note are the oval staircase, the Round Drawing Room and the plaster ceilings. Its site has been associated with the Kennedy family since the late 14th century.

The guest flat is self-contained, comprising several suites, on the top floor of the castle with access by lift. In 1945, lifetime tenure was given to Dwight D. Eisenhower as a Scottish thank you for all the general's wartime work. He certainly did use it on a few occasions including a memorable visit when he was President, but after his death, the Scottish National Trust in association with Scottish Heritage USA made it available to the general public. (An exhibition of Eisenhower's achievements is on permanent display in the public part of the castle.)

Guests in the six-bedroomed flat share the Round Drawing Room, a study and a dining room which seats 16. A kitchenette is equipped for preparing light snacks though breakfast is provided by the resident housekeeper. Linens, tableware, etc. are also supplied. Meals for four people or more can be arranged in the flat and the castle's State Rooms are available for functions.

Culzean is situated in 227 hectares (560 acres) of grounds, Scotland's first country park, which features a 1783 walled garden, a swan pond and the Adam-designed Home Farm whose buildings have been converted to a self-service restaurant, gift shop and information centre. It is located 19 km (12 miles) south of Ayr, off the A719 road, 27 km (17 miles) from Prestwick International Airport.

Maybole, Ayrshire, Scotland. ✆ (06556) 274

6	(the Eisenhower Suite has double/twin beds, bathroom and dressing room, the Ailsa Suite has four poster and en suite bathroom, the Gault and Kennedy Suites are both twin-bedded with en suite bathrooms, the Adam and Cairncross Rooms are twin-bedded with shared bathroom. Rates include supplied breakfast. Two night booking is minimum)
✳	American associations, elegant setting
☞	Arrangements may be made for golfing at Turnberry, Prestwick, Troon and Western Gailes courses. Other leisure activities in the area include sailing, fishing, walking

🏨 Year round

✗ Basically this is a self-catering facility but meals for four people or more can be provided with prior notice when the emphasis is on fresh, home-produced food. Items are available for purchase from a modest cellar stock

♫ No

£/$ A

Dalhousie Castle

Dalhousie Castle, family seat of the Ramsays, has hosted many notable personages in its 800-long years of history. Kings, politicians and lords of the pen have spent time under its roof: Edward I, Henry IV, Oliver Cromwell, Sir Walter Scott, Queen Victoria — have all known its hospitality.

It dates from the 12th century though only the foundations and vaulted dungeons remain from the original structure. The main parts of what you see today were built in the 15th century — from red stone quarried from the opposite river bank of the South Esk — in the form of an L-shaped keep surrounded by an outer wall, a still discernible form, though later additions and modifications have naturally been made. The well at the bottom of the 15th-century drum tower once supplied the castle with all its water — even now its water is drinkable.

In those early years, access to the castle was across a drawbridge over a deep but dry moat. When hotel conversion took place this century, the moat was re-excavated and a new drawbridge constructed but the openings from which castle defenders dropped stones or boiling oil on attackers are original. So is the spiral staircase leading to the small dungeon where prisoners were kept, lowered in by rope as the wall marks attest.

Over the centuries the Ramsay family has contributed to

Scottish history through chivalrous and daring deeds. Their name received royal recognition in 1618 through a Charter granting Sir George Ramsay the title of Lord Ramsay of Dalhousie — his initials are even now visible on the wall of the keep. His brother John was made King James VI's page and his son was raised to Earl of Dalhousie in 1656. There were many splendid achievements for the Ramsays, military and otherwise — the ninth earl, for example, not only was appointed Lt-Governor of Nova Scotia in 1816 but initiated what has since become one of Canada's finest educational establishments, Dalhousie University in Halifax. His youngest son James became President of the Board of Trade when only 33 and three years later the youngest ever Governor-General of India.

Since the turn of this century the Earls of Dalhousie have lived at Brechin while the castle was let to a series of tenants, the present one responsible for its restored luxury. Guest rooms are well appointed and the ancient barrel-vaulted dungeons have been put to excellent use — as an atmospheric candle-lit restaurant where Scottish specialities are served.

Set in 3½ hectares (9 acres) of grounds surrounded by woodland and streams, Dalhousie is perfectly situated for visiting Edinburgh, a 20 minute drive away, or touring the Scottish Borders. Sporting facilities for which Scotland is famous — fishing, golf among them — are all within easy reach.

Bonnyrigg, Edinburgh, Scotland EH19 3JB. ✆ (0875) 20153

24	(some suites; all with en suite bathroom, colour TV)	✳	Peaceful, traditional, historic
🏨	Year round	℘	Many country activities are right on the doorstep: rough shooting on nearby estates, salmon and trout fishing, horse riding, 'dry' skiing, golf at St Andrews, Muirfield, Troon and Gleneagles
✕	An à la carte menu offers the best of Scottish fare: haggis or cock-a-leekie soup for starters perhaps; fresh game in season flambéed with Malt whisky; oatcakes to accompany full flavoured Scottish cheeses		
		♫	No
		£/$	B

Dornoch Castle Hotel

Anyone looking for the romance of castle accommodation, combined with the homeliness of a country house and modern conveniences, will find it at Dornoch Castle Hotel, a dominant landmark on the northern shore of the Dornoch Firth estuary. In fact, this building was originally the 15th-century Palace of the Bishops of Caithness and has since served as garrison, courthouse, jail, school and private residence. (The Earls of Sutherland used it as their home for many years.)

Its most historic features are its tower, dungeons and spiral staircase — all original, but the upper part of the main wing was reconstructed last century and a new wing of bedrooms added in 1974. Today, there is a panelled cocktail bar on the first floor of the tower and what used to be the old Bishop's Palace kitchen has become a pleasant dining room overlooking Dornoch Cathedral.

Dornoch has been privately owned and run by the Ketchin family since 1979, ensuring guest attention is as personal as possible. Thanks to them the Bishop's Room Restaurant has a reputation for being one of the area's best, where 'Taste of Scotland' dishes are a major feature, at prices which won't break the bank.

There are facilities for tennis and bowling but it is golf which is probably the greatest attraction — the Royal

Dornoch Golf Club is a five minute walk from the hotel and is reputed to be Scotland's third oldest as well as one of the finest. Another draw, especially for families, is the beach (a ten minute walk away), noted for its kilometres of sand and bathing.

Though The Dornoch Pipe Band play most summer evenings in front of the castle, don't expect bright lights and action here — it's a place to get away from it all. Sutherland doesn't boast a vast population but instead is a peaceful county silvered with lochs.

Located some 96½ km (60 miles) north of Inverness, Dornoch is a good centre for touring by car. Dunrobin Castle, the Glass Works at Wick, the distillery at Tain and the Salmon Leap at Shin Falls are among the interesting sights in its vicinity.

Dornoch, Sutherland, Scotland IV25 3SD.
✆ (0862) 810216

21 (mostly twin or double, most with private bath or shower, all with coffee/tea trays)	✳ Comfortable rather than impressive, a peaceful summer retreat
🏰 Apr–Oct	℘ Golfing packages are emphasised, using The Royal Dornoch Golf Club which has hosted international championships. Dornoch has tennis and bowling facilities; pony trekking is a few kilometres away. Loch and sea fishing in abundance in the area
✕ Value-for-money fixed-price menus feature fresh produce and change daily. Local fish (Kyle of Sutherland salmon or Lochinver sole) is always a choice. Snack lunches are also available	
	♫ Pipe band most summer evenings in front of castle
	£/$ C

Dromoland Castle

For three centuries the ancestral home of the royal O'Brien clan, Dromoland is a peacefully luxurious castle hotel within easy reach of Shannon airport and many famous Irish landmarks, like Bunratty Castle, after which the very first (15th century) O'Brien property was patterned as a defensive stronghold.

Although the second residential castle built in Queen Anne's time was pulled down in 1811 to make way for the Gothic-styled, stone-walled and towered structure one sees today, many reminders of earlier times still exist. Among the treasured portraits of bygone O'Brien lords and ladies, that still adorn the castle's interior, is one of Donough O'Brien, King of Limerick and Thomond in the 13th century and painted in the 17th century by the Master, Jan Van Wyck. It hangs opposite the reception desk in the front hall near a full length painting of Queen Anne in coronation robes, herself a relative of the O'Brien clan.

The ornamental stone gateway at the entrance of Dromoland's walled rose garden was built in 1648 for Conor and Mary Mahon O'Brien (better known as 'Red Mary'), whilst Queen Anne Court, a courtyard flanked now by guest accommodation and connected to the main building by a carpeted corridor, was originally built by Sir Edward O'Brien in 1736.

Famine, hard times, revolution and war eventually forced the sale of Dromoland's tenant farms and made it increasingly difficult for the O'Briens to finance their 609-hectare (1500-acre) estate. By the time the 20th-century Sir Donough O'Brien (16th Baron of Inchiquin) took over, he was hard-pressed enough to try his hand at dairy farming and later taking in paying guests.

It was an American, however, who converted the establishment to a luxury hotel in 1962 when he bought the castle plus 162 hectares (400 acres) of grounds, hunting and fishing rights. Bernard McDonough, a West Virginian industrialist (but grandson of an Irish immigrant brought in American designers and architects for the remodelling. He added modern heating, plumbing, electrical wiring and restored faded artworks. Working to old landscaping plans, the gardens were redeveloped but with the addition of a golf course.

Today, Lord Inchiquin's octagonal-shaped study under the round tower is a pleasing lounge bar and his library, part of the dining room. But Drumoland has lost none of its stateliness nor the friendly hospitality associated with a family home. It is no wonder that its cuisine (continental with a special Irish touch), its fine wine cellar and its atmosphere (elegant but unstuffy) has attracted entertainers and presidents.

The estate has its own bridle paths and tennis facilities, river and lake for fishing or boating. A popular walk for guests leads to Hermit's Cave, a curious grotto perhaps once used as a smoke house and a nearby domed temple erected in the early 18th century to mark the burial place of the then lord's favourite race horse. Also on the grounds is the hilltop ring fort of Moughaun, believed to have once been a Bronze Age settlement.

Located a 15 minute drive from Shannon airport and an hour from Galway, Dromoland is well sited for day trips to Cork and Blarney Castle, Killarney of the Lakes and Cashel. Ireland's oldest city, Limerick, is 27 km (17 miles) away and neither Bunratty Castle nor Knappogue Castle (both famed for their medieval feasts) are more than 16 km (10 miles).

Newmarket-on-Fergus, County Clare, Ireland.
✆ Shannon 71144

65	(all with en suite bathroom)	✳	Elitist
🏨	Year round	℗	Golf, tennis, croquet,
✗	Native Irish fare—salmon and trout, Dublin Bay prawns		swimming, boating and fishing all on the grounds. Riding stables at nearby Newmarket-on-Fergus
		♫	No
		£/$	B

Fernie Castle

Turreted and crenellated Fernie Castle has been brought firmly from the 14th century to the 20th as a small luxury hotel. Records show that in 1353 it belonged to the Earl of Fife, Duncan the 13th; that in the 15th century it was held by the Fernie family and in the 16th century by the Arnotts. In 1680 the Balfours of Burleigh became the owners, their descendants remaining so until 1965.

During the 18th-century Jacobite rising, Colonel John Balfour's estates were confiscated for his active support of the rebels, but they were later returned to his brother who served in the government forces. The duties of Forester of Falkland and Constable of Cupar have always been associated with the Fernie Barony.

The castle, built on an L plan, has many subsequent alterations but you can still see the 16th-century fortalice and the circular watch tower added some time later. Also of interest, at the back of the castle, is the original lead bath and ice house.

Public rooms are comfortable rather than opulent — a favourite is the stone-vaulted cellar bar. Furnishings are neat and practical — the most special bedroom is the honeymoon suite which boasts a spa bath.

Set in 11 hectares (27 acres) of grounds with a private loch, that is home to ducks and swans, and walking trails, Fernie's management can arrange shooting and fishing locally. Eight famous golf courses are within driving distance, including St Andrews. The hotel is situated on the A914, 6½ km (4 miles) west of Cupar.

Ladybank, Letham, Cupar, Fife, Scotland KY7 7RU.
℘ **(033 781) 381**

16	(mostly double or twin, all with en suite bathroom, mini bar, trouser press, tea/coffee tray. Rates include full Scottish breakfast)
🏨	Year round
✕	Scottish specialities are served in a quiet intimate dining room.

* Comfortable without excessive frills
℘ Arrangements may be made for shooting and fishing or riding. Ladybank Golf Club is only 3 km (2 miles) away — visitor charges are reasonable. St Andrews Golf Course is a 25 minute drive away; seven others are located within 1–1½ hours' travel time
♫ No
£/$ B

Fitzpatrick's Castle

Though it has only been known as Fitzpatrick's Castle Hotel since the family of that name took up residence in 1971 and began to renovate and expand the property, it has been a grand old manor house since 1741 when it was built for the Mapas family.

If it looks less imposing and castle-like than others it is because it was designed as a residence at a time when the emphasis was on comfort rather than fortification. You'll note therefore that the architecture is 'softer', more practical and ceilings are lower. Only in the last 100 years or so was it ever used as an army garrison — indeed rebel headquarters mentioned in Brendan Behan's memoirs.

Fitzpatrick's has changed hands several times over the centuries — perhaps its most colourful residents being the Warren family during the 1800s, notorious for their smuggling activities, which gave the inhabitants of nearby Dalkey and Killiney villages more than a thing or two to talk about. Later in the 19th century, the Chippendale-Higgin family moved in for a brief period — some evidence of their interest in gardening still remains, even though the original estate of 243 hectares (600 acres) has dwindled to 3½ hectares (9 acres).

It still stands in grounds overlooking Dublin Bay surrounded by the 121-hectare (300-acre) woodland preserve of Killiney Hill, but these days it is the Dublin area's only luxury castle hotel with facilities to suit the most demanding guest. International stars like Peter Ustinov, Rod Taylor, Burt Lancaster and Sean Connery have chosen it as their base for a Dublin visit. Larry Hagman of J.R. 'Dallas' fame took the appropriately named Warren Suite (one of the hotel's choicest) as his accommodation.

There are, in fact, several suites and many of the bedrooms feature four posters, albeit not historic ones — all have remote control colour TVs. A welcome bowl of fruit awaits arriving visitors and a goodnight miniature of Bailey's is there for bedtime.

Whilst there is 24-hour room service, dining elegantly means enjoying the candle-lit Victorian-styled ambience of Truffles Restaurant which offers à la carte suggestions or superb value-for-money table d'hôte. Alternatively, Jester's on the lower ground floor is a grill bar cum nightclub. Watering holes range from a friendly foyer bar to intimate cocktail lounge (for residential guests only) to the dungeon bar with a disco for the younger spirited.

Sporting facilities are concentrated indoors where there's a large heated pool, saunas and squash courts, solarium and beauty salon. There are tennis courts but golfing, riding and fishing facilities are not available on the property.

Located only 14½ km (9 miles) from central Dublin yet just a short drive from the lovely countryside of County Wicklow and within easy proximity of Bunratty Castle for a medieval evening out, the Castle is an excellent base for city sightseers and those who seek more rural pursuits.

Killiney, County Dublin, Ireland. ✆ Killiney 851533

86 (some suites, some with four posters, all with en suite bathroom) plus adjacent timeshare apartments available for short-term let	✳ Modern-mix manor house with convivial atmosphere for all ages
🏠 Year round	🏊 Indoor Olympic-sized pool, tennis, squash. Eight golf courses within 8 km (5 miles)
✗ Fresh game and local seafood are Truffles' specialities. First class steaks in Jester's. Special value tourist menus in both restaurants. Weekday last orders as late as 11 pm	🎵 Music/dancing for all ages
	£/$ B

Glenborrodale Castle

Glenborrodale Castle is so newly converted to a hotel worth taking notice of that, at the time of writing, it wasn't even open yet! But if I tell you that America's Cup yachtsman and international businessman, Peter de Savary, purchased this piece of west coast Scottish Victoriana and has spent £1 million to redecorate and refurbish it, you may realise why it's worth investigating. De Savary is known for turning 'sows' ears into silk purses' and this turn-of-the-century stone pile looks as if it won't be any exception.

Set on the Ardnamurchan Peninsula, overlooking the Isle of Mull and Loch Sunart, mid the purple-hearthered scenery of the Western Highlands, the property was built by C.D. Rudd, a contemporary of Cecil Rhodes and quarter shareholder in De Beers gold mines and diamond fields. He bought the land in 1900 and it only took three years to erect the red sandstoned, towered and parapeted house.

Legend of course dates the site to the earlier times of Norse raiders when the Viking fortress of Caisteal Breac was built here. They say that the overlord of the time was the 2 m (7 ft) tall Borrodale, who despite his strength was killed in a local fight and lies buried on the spot where today's hotel stands.

That story is for you to believe or not. Rudd we do know about and the trees he brought from South Africa are an imposing part of the castle grounds and gardens. For nature lovers, the whole of the region is a paradise from the hills where deer graze to the rocky outcrops off deep bays where seals bask. Mull's picturesque fishing village, Tobermory, is a mere 30 minute boat ride away — the hotel will pack you a picnic and ferry you across for the day — collect you back for dinner of Scottish traditional fare and fruit and vegetables straight from the kitchen garden.

It's not surprising that de Savary fell in love with this place enough to buy it — the Western Isles have always been a magnet for yachtsmen. Sunart is one of the largest sea lochs, 32 km (20 miles) long, and a safe one for visitors. Windsurfers, outboard dinghys and sailing boats are available for hire from Glenborrodale who will also arrange for other sports. The less energetic can settle for the hotel's own croquet lawn or putting green.

Though the hotel's location is a secluded (wildly romantic according to some) one, Glasgow's two main airports are within easy reach and helicopter service cuts time to reach Ardnamurchan to half an hour. Alternatively, hired cars are no problem — the drive from Glasgow takes you past Loch Lomond and through the Pass of Glencoe, or by prior arrangement a chauffeured limousine will pick you up.

Acharacle, Argyll, Scotland PH36 4JP. ✆ **(097) 24266**

16	(including suites, many with four posters, all decorated in traditional Victorian style, all with en suite bathroom and colour TV. Rates include full Scottish breakfast)	✳	Secluded, romantic setting for the sports minded
		℘	The hotel has its own billiard room, solarium and gym, croquet lawn, tennis court, putting green and clay pigeon facilities. Windsurfers, dinghys and sailing boats are available. Arrangements may be made for fishing, trekking and climbing.
🏨	Easter–Oct		
✕	Fruit and vegetables from the hotel's kitchen garden served with traditional Scottish fare like salmon, trout, grouse, pheasant and venison. The oak-panelled Library serves as a bar	♫	No
		£/$	A

Inverlochy Castle

No one writing about grand and stately places to stay would dream of omitting Inverlochy Castle, not only because it is majestic looking set in the equally majestic foothills of Ben Nevis, but because the welcome inside is a warm one.

For the longest time, the estate was the Scarlett family home after the Hon. Robert Campbell Scarlett, second Baron of Abinger, bought the property in 1843. It was his son, William, who built the castle you see today after his marriage to an American, Helen Magruder, in 1863. Their children, who grew up here, were not the only ones to fall in love with the magnificent West Highland scenery — during her 1873 week's stay at the castle, Queen Victoria wrote in her diary: 'I never saw a lovelier or a more romantic spot.'

Once William, now Lord Abinger, had retired from the army in 1877, he spent a great deal of time on the 15,795-hectare (39,000-acre) estate, supervising numerous development programmes and taking an active part in the local community. Even after his death in 1892 and later that of his unmarried son in 1903, other members of the Scarlett family continued to maintain Inverlochy until it was sold to a Canadian in 1944.

The fine Victorian proportions of the public rooms are enhanced by their handsome décor, befitting for an establishment that calls itself 'home' more than a hotel and insists its staff do not accept tips. The Great Hall is particularly attractive with its frescoed ceiling and chandeliers and a staircase that seems to 'cascade' down. The present owners have, of course, modernised to some extent so that there is central heating throughout the en suite bathrooms.

Dining is a merit-worthy experience, indeed the cuisine has won Michelin accolades. Whenever possible, fresh produce from garden, farm, mountain and loch is used to create star-quality dishes. Since the castle cannot accommodate many guests, it is like dining in a wealthy friend's home though there are separate tables. There is no formal menu but individual guests' preferences are catered to. Nor are portions skimpy.

The cellar holds some excellent wines but remember, too, that there's always a supply of pure water from the slopes of Ben Nevis, untouched by chemicals. This same water source is used to distil the famous 'Dew of Ben Nevis' whisky.

The castle's own 20 hectares (50 acres) of grounds, smothered with rhododendrons and surrounded by 200 hectares (500 acres) of farmland, are a delight in themselves but there are many beauty spots in the area which may be visited, including the Isle of Skye and Loch Lomond. Given advance notice, chauffeured cars can be provided for touring, and by arrangement guests can be met at Glasgow's airport, 160 km (99 miles) away or at other Scottish airports and railway stations.

Torlundy, Fort William, Scotland PH33 6SN.
✆ **(0397) 2177**

16	(including 2 suites, all with en suite bathroom and colour TV. Rates include a full Scottish breakfast)	✳	Inverlochy permeates a cosy family style of hospitality in a peacefully serene region of Scotland
🏨	Mid March–mid Nov	♂	Fair — there is an all-weather tennis court on the grounds and trout fishing on a nearby private loch. Horse riding and golf courses are within easy driving distance
✕	Cooking is delicious and portions generous for a fixed price dinner. Light lunches are available on request		
		♫	No
		£/$	A

Kilravock Castle

Historically, this castle is a gem, filled with mementoes of the Rose Clan, whose family home it has been since 1490; it has been taking paying guests since 1967. Ancestral portraits hang everywhere — in the hallways, the drawing room, the dining room. Kilravock the Seventh (15th century), for example, is one of those gracing the dining room, along with Kilravock the Eighth. The dark-complexioned Kilravock the Tenth (Black Baron) of the 16th century is displayed in the hall; two of Kilravock the Fifteenth's wives on the stairs.

Paintings are not the only visible evidence of bygone eras: the pikes and chainmail shirts decorating the hall more than likely date to the Battle of Bannockburn (1314), while the boots in the fireplace at the entrance hall are certainly relics of the Battle of Culloden. The lute on view in one of the drawing room cabinets belonged to Elizabeth Rose of Kilravock (18th century) who entertained Robert Burns here during his visit in 1787. And the punch bowl and drinking cup are survivors of the time when Kilravock entertained Bonnie Prince Charlie.

Architecturally, the tower is the oldest part, the mansion house section being added in 1553. The main staircase, corridors and west wing were added during the 18th century, as were the powdering closets seen in the corner of the red, blue, bee and yellow rooms. Inscriptions on the castle walls relate to different periods in its history: the stone plaque which reads 'Non est salus nisi in Christo. Solo Deo

Gloria' (There is no salvation except in Christ. To God alone be glory) was what William Rose placed on a bridge he opened at Nairn in 1631. That above the fireplace in the old dining hall (now used for Sunday evening buffets) is a quotation from Hugh Rose's own book, written when minister of Nairn (1660–1686).

Traditionally, the Roses have always been a religious family. In 1220 High Rose had a chapel built at Geddes and at Kilravock itself a private chapel was put into the central floor of the castle tower. Today the castle is run as an Interdenominational Christian Guest House, on a non-profit-making basis. It is unlicensed, and if you're not one for breakfast and dinner Bible readings, then perhaps you may be best off elsewhere. But guests won't find this place sombre and there are extensive grounds in which to wander. The tree garden, woodland and nature trails are peaceful and Nairn's sandy beach is nor far away. The River Nairn runs along the border of the estate, and may be fished by prior arrangement. The village of Croy is a 1½km (1 mile) walk away.

Located 19km (12 miles) east of Inverness (6½ km, four miles, from the airport), and 9½ km (6 miles) west of Nairn, Kilravock boasts a central position in the Scottish Highlands. Many castles are situated nearby, like Cawdor and Brodie, along with Culloden Battlefield. The Kessock Bridge across the Moray Firth allows places like the Kyle of Lochalsh to be reached in just over two hours' drive.

Croy, Inverness, Scotland IV1 2PJ. ✆ (06678) 258

---

20 (mostly family sized, all with coffee/tea trays but only some with en suite bathroom. Most historic rooms are in the main part of the castle. Rates are for bed & breakfast or half board)	✳ Homely and temperant!
	℘ Fair. The castle has its own squash court, tennis court, putting green and croquet. Horse riding is available nearby. Fishing in part of the River Nairn by arrangement. Closest golf courses are at Nairn.
🏨 Apr–Oct	
✗ Varied menu, liberal portions. No bar	♫ No
	£/$ C

Langley Castle

They say that Langley Castle is England's only remaining medieval fortified castle hotel. Without doubt, its 2m (7ft) thick walls provide an exclusive refuge from which to explore Northumbria. It was built in 1350 during Edward III's reign and despite numerous owners over the centuries has managed to maintain what architects would call 'integrity'. It should come as no surprise that this is a Grade 1 Listed Building, especially since the main staircase houses what are considered the finest remaining examples of 14th-century garderobes in Europe.

By the 17th century, the Langley Estates were the property of the Earls of Derwentwater (for whom one of the guest rooms is currently named). After the Jacobite rebellion in which James, the third Earl, and his brother Charles took part — and were subsequently executed — the Crown confiscated the estate until 1882. Historian, Cadwallader Bates, purchased it and together with his wife Josephine set out to restore it. Each is remembered by a room name. After her husband's death it was Josephine who rebuilt the original chapel in the castle roof in memory to him.

Though Langley only has eight bedrooms, each has individuality both in décor and amenities. The Josephine Room, for example, features a jacuzzi bath while The Radcliffe Room boasts its own sauna, and The Derwentwater Room, a canopied bed. An open fireplace and beautiful stained glass windows give the drawing room character —

the place to relax with a drink from the adjoining oak-panelled bar.

Indeed, Langley, set in 4 hectares (10 acres) of wooded grounds, is a place to relax, get away from it all, not one for rebel raisers these days. The surrounding unspoilt countryside will be best enjoyed by those who like to ramble. At the doorstep of Hadrian's Wall and its Roman forts, Langley is located 9½ km (6 miles) from Hexham on the verge of Northumberland's National Park, 32 km (20 miles) from Newcastle airport.

Langley-on-Tyne, Hexham, Northumberland, England NE47 5LU. ✆ (0434 84) 8888

8	(all individually furnished but all with en suite bathroom and colour TV. Prices vary according to special features such as sauna, jacuzzi bath or canopied bed)	✳	Traditional British food and innovative dishes are served in the small restaurant
	Year round	℘	There's nothing laid on, though fishing and shooting can be arranged
✕	Tranquil, relaxing and intimate.	♫	No
		£/$	C

Lumley Castle

No wonder Lumley Castle is said to be haunted! There's a maze of passages and spiral staircases leading to various function and public rooms; stone-flagged floors and high-beamed ceilings. This well-preserved 13th-century castle — origins go back to the 9th century — has been consistently refurbished over the years to become a hotel of international repute without losing its atmosphere. And the ghost? That was Lily of Lumley, the castle's most famous resident, said to have haunted the building ever since she met an untimely death at the hands of religious opposers in the late 1300s.

The ancestral home of the Earls of Scarborough, Lumley's most visible historic features for today's guests include a genuine Queen Anne four poster bed in the King James' Suite, just one of the castle feature guest rooms, each of which is unique. Medieval pillars support a multi-domed ceiling in the Black Knight restaurant, romantically candle-lit at night, while a giant stone fireplace dominates the splendid baronial hall, setting for Elizabethan banquets when as many as 200 revellers feast and drink, attended by 'Ladies of the Court'.

Hotel guests are welcome to browse through any of the 3,000 books lining the walls of the library bar, play a game of snooker in the Billiards Room, or explore the secret passages. In keeping with modern times, Lumley has converted former stables to bedrooms and offers its own sauna and outdoor swimming pool.

Set in 2½ hectares (6 acres) of parkland overlooking and adjoining golf course and the River Wear, this castle hotel is an ideal base from which to discover Northumbria's ancient kingdom. Situated between the cities of Durham and Newcastle, a three minute drive from the A1, it features weekend breaks and special themed weekends.

Chester-le-Street, Co. Durham, England DH3 4NX.
✆ (0385) 891111

52   (12 single, 36 double and twin, 3 four posters and 1 suite, all except nine have private bath or shower; castle rooms have the most character. All feature colour TV, trouser press and tea/coffee-making facilities)

🏨   Year round

✗   Fine wines and food combine with first class service in the Black Knight restaurant and adjacent bar. Menu is 'international'

✳   Impressive — a blend of modern comfort and bygone images

𝒫   Fair. Sauna and outdoor pool within the property, golf course adjacent to the grounds. Many walks in the grounds, woodlands and along the river bank

♫   Elizabethan banquets most days of the week, bookable in advance. Ample servings of mead and wine accompany a five course meal with choral and other entertainment

£/$ C

Pennsylvania Castle Hotel

All Americans will be familiar with the name of this hotel given in honour of Sir William Penn, founder of Pennsylvania, by his grandson Governor John Penn in 1800. King George III, a frequent visitor to the Island of Portland, was the first to suggest it was built and it was later occupied for many years by his daughter, Princess Elizabeth. Designed with towers and battlements by James Wyatt, the castle overlooks secluded Church Ope Cove, once a landing place for smugglers ferrying brandy across the English Channel.

Thomas Hardy modelled Sylvania Castle in his novel *The Well Beloved* on this property which is still the official meeting place of the Court Leet of Portland, instituted originally in 872 by King Alfred. The Isle of Portland, nicknamed 'Gibraltar of Wessex' by Hardy, is unique, a rocky limestone peninsula connected by a stretch of shingle known as Chesil Bank.

Today Pennsylvania is a family-run hotel still displaying the flag of the Commonwealth of Pennsylvania, presented by the United States Senate, in its hall. In the Round Tower is the residents' lounge plus a circular cocktail bar. The bright and airy Georgian Restaurant features table d'hôte meals and an à la carte selection.

Set in a sub-tropical garden from which a footpath leads to a shingle beach, Pennsylvania Castle is within easy distance of many historic places of interest. Corfe Castle is one, the ancestral home of the Bond family who were related by marriage to George Washington and from whose family crest it is believed the Stars and Stripes were first taken. The county town of Dorchester where weekly markets and horse sales are held, is a mere 16 km (10 miles) away.

Situated at the southern end of the Island of Portland, 2½ km (1½ miles) from famous Portland Bill, the hotel is 11 km (7 miles) from Weymouth which has a direct train link with London.

Portland, Dorset, England DT5 1HZ. ✆ **(0305) 820561**

12

🏨 Year round

✗ The chef de cuisine has a good reputation for à la carte dishes like Piccata Tessinoise, Emince Zurichoise and Paupiettes de boeuf au vin rouge. Bar snacks are available in the Tavern Bistro. Special rates on food for children

✳ Convivial friendly atmosphere where families are especially made welcome

℘ Riding, golf, fishing and sailing may be arranged through the hotel

♫ No

£/$ C

Ruthin Castle

Like the Welsh themselves, despite its turreted and somewhat glowering appearance, Ruthin Castle is a homely welcoming place to stay. A royal one, too, for it was built originally by Edward I between 1282 and 1284. A much later Edward (the VII) was also a regular visitor here when he was Prince of Wales, attending distinguished gatherings hostessed by the Victorian-era-owner, Lady Cornwallis-West.

In between and since, the castle has changed face and owners several times. The original building, destroyed by Oliver Cromwell, was resurrected in 1796. Additions were made in 1849, 1887 and again in 1922. From a fortress which had seen medieval, stormy times, like the unsuccessful 1400 siege by Owain Glynowr, it had become a noble family home.

Ruthin was turned into a hotel in 1963 but its bygone years have not all been forgotten as you'll note from the oak-panelled entrance hall adorned with old weapons and pewter. The inner hall is dominated by a painting of Lady Cornwallis-West and, dating much farther back, are the 13th-century ruins in the grounds which boast not only dungeons but a drowning pool and whipping pit!

Those 15 hectares (38 acres) of gardens and parkland lend a peaceful air yet the centre of the medieval market town of Ruthin is only a three minute walk away — where you'll find a craft centre among other shops selling local goods. Anyone with a car and a yen for outdoor sports will find facilities nearby. Its location makes it an ideal vacation base for exploring Wales' cultural and historic heritage: the Roman town of Chester is only 35 km (22 miles) away and Caernarvon Castle, site of the investiture of the Prince of Wales, 80 km (50 miles). This gateway to Snowdonia is also about an hour's drive from Manchester airport.

One of the main delights for tourists staying at Ruthin is the Medieval Feast it features almost daily. The evening starts with a welcome reception and continues with a four course banquet accompanied by mead and wine drunk from pewter goblets. Entertainment is offered by the 'Ladies of the Court' who sing in both Welsh and English, to the strings of a harp.

Ruthin, Clwyd, Wales, LL15 2NU.
✆ Ruthin (08242) 2664

60	(including 1 with four poster; all with en suite bathroom, colour TV and complimentary tea/coffee trays). Dogs can stay for small charge
▥	Year round
✗	Reasonable but not exotic fare, table d'hôte and à la carte, served in a 100-seat restaurant. Cocktail bar in the library. Medieval Banquet must be booked in advance

✳	Period appeal but unstuffy, informal — good family choice
℘	None on site but tennis, mountain walks, pony trekking and trout fishing on the River Clywd all within easy reach. The Pwllglas 9-hole golf course is a 5 minute ride away.
♫	Medieval Feast almost daily. Bookable in advance; it's great fun for a one-off evening
£/$	B

Stobo Castle Health Spa

Unique in the world of castle hotels, Stobo is a marvellous health resort with a historic past. The Manor of Stobo dates back more than 1000 years though the present building was erected in 1805 under architectural instruction to be 'all right in baronial style' for the then Lord Chief Baron, Sir James Montgomery. Over a century later, famous test cricketer Hylton Philipson extended the terraces, created a lake stocked with trout and the Japanese Water Garden. More recently, the Winyard family gave it the image for fitness.

Inside the crenellated and towered castle the panelled Great Hall and the exquisite mouldings in other public rooms are of greatest architectural interest — furnishings spell luxury. Guests of course come here to be pampered in the healthiest possible way. Anyone can use the indoor heated pool and many of the beauty treatments are included in the tariff. Whether in a holiday plan or costed as extras, a full range is available from saunas, steam and spa baths, G5 and underwater massage to Cathiodermie Aromatherapy, Paraffin waxing, Parafango and Algotherapy. Stobo will also plan personal beauty programmes that could include a facial and new hairdo.

Daily exercise programmes are also part of the package; relaxation and self defence classes are given once a week.

Hair and beauty demonstrations are frequently given at the spa; so are cooking demonstrations in the chef's kitchen. Sporting facilities on the grounds include cycling and tennis or guests may join the guided walks and nature trails.

One of the most pleasant areas for private contemplation is the Japanese Water Gardens, tucked away in the wooded parkland, a tranquil beautifully landscaped area.

Stobo may primarily be concerned with weight and centimetres but that doesn't have to mean muscle overkill and a strict regime of lemon juice. Diets are prepared for those who wish to lose weight, gain it or merely enjoy well balanced meals, as well as those with a special preference like vegetarian. The castle very clearly states it is no medical centre.

Located 43 km (27 miles) south of Edinburgh and a little more from Glasgow, Stobo is a place to stay in, not to roam from, if you are to take advantage of what it offers.

Peeblesshire, Scotland EH45 8NY. ✆ 07216 249

25	(single and twin, all individually and elegantly furnished; most with en suite bathroom; all with colour television)	✳	Fashionable for the fitness conscious
🏛	Year round	℘	Full health club facilities. Tennis and cycling on the grounds. Arrangements may be made for fly and coarse fishing, game shooting, horse riding and golf
✗	Local farm produce is much in evidence — Scottish salmon and game, fresh fruits and vegetables, imaginatively prepared, stylishly presented. All types of diets available. As much tea and coffee as you like all day long. The hotel's pure water is piped from Stobo's own freshwater spring	♬	No
		£/$	A

Thornbury Castle

Once owned by Henry VIII (yes he and Anne Boleyn did sleep here!), Thornbury Castle is said to be the only Tudor castle/palace remaining in England. Originally, Thornbury was but a manor (early accounts date it from the 10th century) which was granted to Robert Fitzhamon by William Rufus when he came to the throne in 1087, as a reward for supporting him, and was then passed down through generations of Staffords.

It was Edward Stafford, third Duke of Buckingham, who started to build the present castle in 1508, copying Henry VII's idea for a castle which wasn't a fortress. The duke continued to stay in favour under Henry VIII, battling side by side with the king at the battle of the Spurs in Picardy and holding the highest rank of office. But a few indiscreet words and a steward's revenge got the better of him and later that century he was arrested and executed. Henry VIII appropriated the castle and enjoyed it for 33 years. Mary Tudor also spent some years here under the tutelage of the Bishop of Exeter, and when she became queen she returned the castle to Henry Lord Stafford, Buckingham's son, in 1554.

Evidence of Tudor times is still to be seen even though for two centuries Thornbury fell into neglected disrepair. Over the main gateway is an inscription showing when work started and the Duke of Buckingham's motto 'Doresenavent' (old fashioned French for 'henceforward'), plus the family coat of arms. Badges over the gatehouse and on windows or fireplace inside the castle show The Stafford Knot, the mantle of Brecknock, the Antelope of Bohun, the Swan of Essex and the Fiery Axle of Woodstock. The elaborate brick double chimney on the south side is unequalled — the most similar being at Hampton Court, while only Windsor Castle still boasts oriel windows of the type to be seen here.

The hotel retains all the character of its former life, filled with artworks and period pieces. Drinks are taken in The Library (surrounded by real books) or The Drawing Room, particularly cosy when warmed by winter fires. Each guest bedroom is uniquely decorated: Anne Boleyn stayed in what is now The Duke's Bedchamber, a large octagonal room featuring a canopied bed with mirrored ceiling; No. 9, now a single bedroom, once stored the ladies' jewels and has beautiful views through leaded windows of the castle gardens.

Fine food is very much a factor at Thornbury but smoking is not allowed in the atmospheric dining rooms. The castle's own vineyards produces some exceptionally passable white wine with which to accompany cuisine that has been recipient of numerous awards.

One of the disused buildings in the grounds may yet be due for restoration — it has been historically vetted and authenticated as England's oldest Tudor tennis court, but could well become a banqueting hall. With or without it, Thornbury's setting, surrounded by manicured gardens, high walls and views over the Severn into Gloucestershire and Wales, is blissful.

Located close to Bristol, 8 km (5 miles) from the Severn Bridge and the junctions of the M4 and M5 motorways, the hotel is well placed for touring the West Country.

Thornbury, Bristol, England BS12 1HH.
✆ (0454) 412647

18	(mostly twin or double, some with four posters, all with individual décor; all with en suite bathroom and colour TV. Complimentary sherry awaits guests. Luxury amenities include fluffy bathrobes, trouser press, hairdryer and wooden toilet seats. No children under 12)	✳	Lots of Tudor character. Quiet private baronial home style
		℘	Riding, golf; shooting may be arranged
🏨	Year round, except for Christmas	♫	No
✗	French, with imaginative flair	£/$	A

The Tregenna Castle Hotel

Tregenna Castle Hotel is what it looks to be — an 18th-century miniature castle. Its imposing position on top of St Ives' tallest hills gives it commanding views of St Ives Bay. It deserves its place in this book more for its range of facilities than the stories it might tell.

Comfort without fuss is the key in this family suited hotel. Public and guest rooms are pleasant; a proper Cornish cream tea just one of the irresistible meals to be enjoyed here. Tregenna comes especially into its own with its outdoor recreational facilities, surrounded as it is by 28 hectares (70 acres) of parkland. On the grounds a heated pool not only provides pleasure for swimmers and sun-bathers but has magnificent views of the bay below. For mild exercise, a gentle game of croquet doesn't go amiss; for the more energetic there are badminton, squash and tennis courts. The hotel also boasts its own 18-hole golf course.

Unlike Cornwall's northwest coast of dramatic cliffs, St Ives Bay is a sheltered cove with golden beaches. St Ives itself is a popular, photogenic bustling fishing village of winding lanes and little cottages, located only about 1 km (½ mile) from Tregenna.

Situated as it is, 48 km (30 miles) from Newquay airport, on the A3074 between Lelant and St Ives, this is a perfect centre for a stay-put holiday or an excellent base for touring

Cornwall. To the south, St Michael's Mount may be reached on foot at low tide; farther on is Penzance, departure point for the Scilly Isles.

St Ives, Cornwall, England TR26 2DE. ✆ (0736) 795254

| 84 | (9 single, 10 double, 65 twin; almost all with private bathroom, all with colour TV, baby listening service and tea/coffee tray) |

🏨 Mar–Oct

✕ International and local food with fresh seafood a regular menu feature. Regional specialities include lobster, crab and mackerel. Children's menus available

✳ Convivial, well suited to families

🏌 Good. In the grounds, a heated swimming pool, 3 hard and 3 grass tennis courts, croquet and an 18-hole par 3 golf course. Also facilities for badminton and squash. Riding may be arranged through local stables and the waters off St Ives are suitable for surfing, waterskiing and even shark fishing! Walking along Cornwall's coastal cliff paths is another popular pastime

♫ No

£/$ B

Waterford Castle

Always a castle but very newly a hotel, Waterford Castle is a romantic exclusive retreat which only opened its doors to the general public in 1988. Originally built around the time of the Anglo-Norman invasion by Richard de Clare, Earl of Pembroke (nicknamed 'Strongbow'), it was more latterly the 19th-century Irish home of writer Edward Fitzgerald who no doubt hosted his friends Thackeray, Tennyson and Carlyle under this very roof on more than one occasion. Until ten years ago, it was home to Italian Princess Caracciolo, one of his descendants.

Tree-bordered avenues lead to the handsome and imposing stone building faced with ancient gargoyles. Who can fail to be impressed by the Great Hall beneath the main tower with its arched Portland stone walls rising to a finely plastered ceiling, and its Elizabethan oak panelling. When winter calls for a fire, logs are brought in from the surrounding estate to burn comfortably in the giant stone fireplace.

The dining room is considered one of the finest of its kind in Ireland for its magnificent full Elizabethan oak panelling, an ornate plastered ceiling and a carved oak fireplace which features the Fitzgerald crest. Much of the food served here comes from the 125-hectare (310-acre) island estate — organically grown vegetables and fruit from the 2 hectares (5 acres) of glasshouses, organically fed lamb, cattle and deer.

Guest bedrooms as you might expect have modern conveniences but are individually designed in keeping with the castle's age. Those completed are reached by a fine carved staircase but eventually there will be more accommodation in the courtyard.

Situated on the River Suir, only 2½ km (1½ miles) downstream from Waterford City, home of the famous cut crystal, the island is reached by the castle's own chain-linked driven ferry. The island itself is large enough to provide recreational facilities like shooting and horse riding and its own shore is good for salmon and trout fishing, but there are many other things to do and places to see within the vicinity. The castle is located 5 km (3 miles) from Waterford's airport, 72 km (45 miles) from Rosslare and 153 km (95 miles) from Shannon.

The Island, Ballinakill, Waterford, Ireland.
✆ (051) 78203

---

19 (12 deluxe, 2 standard, 5 executive suites; all with four poster bed, en suite bathroom. Rates include full Irish breakfast)

🏨 All year

✕ Fresh organically produced fruit and vegetables are the basis for menus. Also organically fed lamb, deer and cattle. Good wine cellar

✳ The old/new combination make a special retreat

𝒫 First class. The castle boasts its own indoor heated pool and a tennis court. On the estate pheasant and duck shooting are available in season; clay pigeon shooting at other times. In addition to salmon and trout fishing from the island shore, there are nearby deep sea angling facilities. Horse and pony riding are available year round — polo can be played at Whitfield Court, 5 km (3 miles) away. Castle guests may play golf at Waterford's 18-hole course or that at Tramore, 16 km (10 miles) away. Watersports can be enjoyed at nearby beaches.

♫ No

£/$ A

ITALY

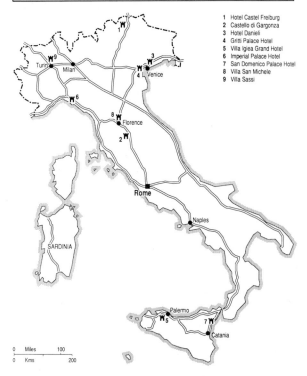

1 Hotel Castel Freiburg
2 Castello di Gargonza
3 Hotel Danieli
4 Gritti Palace Hotel
5 Villa Igiea Grand Hotel
6 Imperial Palace Hotel
7 San Domenico Palace Hotel
8 Villa San Michele
9 Villa Sassi

There are many splendidly grandiose hotels in Italy but only a few which genuinely have been palazzi in a previous age. The ones selected for this book are luxury ones, recommended for style and service, mostly operated by Italian chains with top bracket hotel know-how and US/UK representation. Indeed, just looking at CIGA hotels, one was very tempted to include the likes of the Grand in Rome, the Excelsior in Florence and the Principe di Savoia in Milan for their pure olde-worlde glamour.

We have included a number of the villa conversions which abound in Italy, many of them very beautiful places to stay in peaceful country settings. As elsewhere, these would formerly have been private homes of the wealthy, often left neglected for years before a commercially minded person with an entrepreneurial gleam in his eye set his sights on them.

Italy's exceptional history has bestowed it with monuments and its craftsmen have left us superb examples of their work. We would be particularly happy to receive comments on any historic villa hotel not so far included.

Hotel Castel Freiberg

The medieval character of Castel Freiberg, with its square tower and fortified walls, has scarcely changed over the ages. There is still a chapel inside, consecrated to the Holy Cross as a religious institution from the Middle Ages. There are even two rooms with walls from the year 1000.

The first documented evidence of a castle here is in the 14th century when it was called 'Tifrags'. In the 15th century, during the ownership by the wealthy Niederthor family, it was enlarged — the Renaissance Gallery and the wood-panelled Baronial Hall have remained in perfect condition to this day. Over the years, Freiberg has known many an owner — counts and barons until it became a hotel, an Italian member of the prestigious Relais et Châteaux consortium.

Some of the décor is rustic: whitewashed walls, tiled floors, beamed ceilings; some is glamorous with rich wood-work. Guests use the basement taverna as a club room and dine upstairs. On the ground floor is an indoor swimming pool, gym and massage room plus small beauty salon, along with other public rooms. A 15th-century staircase leads to the upper floor dining rooms and vaulted reading room — also to six balconied guest rooms. Most of the bedrooms, however, are on the second floor.

Merano is 25 km (15½ miles) from Bolzano which may be

reached by a picturesque route or by a new highway. As a tourist centre the town has a casino and thermal centre and is planning a golf course. On the hotel's own grounds is an outdoor pool and tennis court.

Via Labers, 39012 Merano, Italy. ✆ **(0473) 44196**

36	(including suites; all with en suite bathroom, TV and built-in safe)	✳	Quietly elegant
	🏨 Apr–Nov	℘	Indoor and outdoor pool, gym, massage parlour, games room. Tennis court, table tennis and opportunities for walks in the surrounds
✕	Italian with Relais style		
		♫	No
		£/$	

Castello di Gargonza

Castello di Gargonza is atypical of a castle hotel — it is a restored 13th-century walled village in the Tuscan hills between Arezzo and Siena, overlooking the Chiana Valley. The first wayfarer to head this way was reputedly Dante in 1304 when the exiled poet was thought to be with the Ghibellines. But don't expect a stack of Dante memorabilia — it simply doesn't exist.

What does exist for this decade's wayfarers is the turreted and towered castle, a modest Romanesque church and 20 red-roofed, stone cottages, charmingly renovated within the walls. Count Roberto Guicciardini and his wife have made their conversion with the usual excellent Italian flair — each beamed and rustic casa is individually decorated to retain its 13th-century character but all boast the modern conveniences of bathrooms, kitchens and heating. Guests can rent them by the week for a self-catering holiday, or by the night as a hotel — there is a restaurant in the complex, serving interesting Tuscan fare.

From the sunken garden with its fig trees and pots of petunias and geraniums you can see the hills beyond. Many of the houses, too, have lovely views of the lush vine-clad valley, the forest and woodlands. Casa Palle, for example, has its own open terrace and Casa Fonteblanda 1 has access to two pigeon towers for a bird's eye view.

Gargonza has been in the Guicciardini family for some 400 years, its cottages the homes of those who tended the vineyards. More recently, though, hard times suggested the risk of its becoming a ghost town — hence the hotel it is today.

There are no shops here so self-caterers must stock up in Monte San Savino. Houses are equipped with linens, towels, cutlery and dishes but not dishwashers; breakfast and maid service is available. The restaurant, just outside the walls, is designed in similar fashion to the cottages with a beamed ceiling, tiled floor and a stone archway leading to a terrace for meals al fresco in warm weather. You may miss a pool (though one is planned), but the surrounding towns and scenery are well worth seeing and their atmosphere is genuinely Italian — a far cry from the touristy resorts. The castello is located 8 km (5 miles) from Monte San Savino, 35 km (22 miles) from Siena.

Monte San Savino, Gargonza 52048, Arezzo, Italy.
℃ (0575) 847021

▭ 20 separate houses with from one to three bedrooms (all with kitchen, bathroom and living room — often with fireplace)	✱ Uniquely Tuscan
	℘ No, but large grounds and pool planned
▦ Feb–Dec	♫ No
✕ Specialities include wild boar, assorted roast meats, pasta Tuscan style, and the local red and white wine of Castello di Gargonza and Vin Santo	£/$

Hotel Danieli

During the 14th and 15th centuries, everyone who was anyone owned a palazzo in Venice, but none was more beautiful nor so well positioned — in Calle delle Razze, overlooking Riva degli Schiavoni — than Palazzo Dandolo, built for Doge Enrico Dandolo. Today — the Hotel Danieli.

At the time of its initial construction, the Venetian Senate encouraged the sumptuous, the more splendid the better, as an example of Venetian power — to lodge and show off to visiting nobility and ambassadors. Both façades and interiors therefore matched in magnificence, and in the case of Palazzo Dandolo, a gold staircase led from the inner courtyard to the first and second floors.

Given the number of titled families in Italy in those days, and their power struggles, it was inevitable that this palace should change hands several times — from the Dandolo family to the Grittis, then the Mocenigos and after that, the Bernardos, but happily each family did its utmost to preserve its opulence.

When the Venetian Republic fell, however, the property was split up among various families and it wasn't until Guiseppe Dal Niel set his ambitious sights on the place that it had hopes of regaining former glory. But this time as a hotel. He began his project in 1822 by renting it; later bought the second floor from Alviso Bernardo's widow; and eventually purchased the first floor in 1840 from the then Mocenigo heir. Only then did he give it his own name or nickname — Danieli, prefacing it with 'Royal' to remind guests it had always been a lodging fit for kings.

Throughout the 19th century staying at the Royal Danieli added to a visitor's prestige. The hotel continued to welcome royalty like King William of Prussia but equally attracted the artistically minded. Dickens, Wagner, Balzac and Proust have in their time all signed the guest book here and the Danieli was the 1833–1884 setting for George Sand's love affair with Alfred De Musset. (Their corner room, now No. 10, is constantly in demand by the romantic)

What you see and experience today was made possible when Compagnia Italiana Grandi Alberghi (CIGA) took over at the beginning of this century. They restored the 19th-century Casanuova section and added the Danielino wing behind the oldest part of the palace. Air conditioning and other modern amenities were installed to ensure there was 20th-century comfort along with Byzantine charm. No, there isn't a swimming pool or health club (though private launches will transport guests to the nearby Venice Lido's beaches and watersports, tennis courts and golf courses). Nor, since Venice is a network of canals, is there parking space, but there is a garage in Piazzale Roma and private launch transfer to and from the airport. There is, however, a beauty salon, baby sitting and business services. And atmosphere!

Located literally a few minutes' walk from St Mark's Square, bordered by famous monuments like the Doge's Palace, the Danieli is perfect for exploring the heart of Venice. Its Terrazza restaurant, too, open to the sky in summer, offers an exceptional panorama to all who choose to dine there.

Riva Schiavoni 4196, 30122 Venezia, Italy.
✆ **(041) 5226480**

238	(predominantly double but many single and some suites; some balconied, some terraced; all with en suite bathroom, colour TV; mini bars on request)	✳	Tops for those who appreciate historic architecture and wondrous chandeliers
		℘	Beach and water sports at sister hotel, Venice Lido
🏨	Year round	♫	No
✗	Regional Venetian specialities in Terrazza restaurant for dining with a view. Snack service in Dandolo bar	£/$	A

Gritti Palace Hotel

When you are a guest in a doge's house, you have every right to expect royal treatment. The Hotel Gritti Palace, built for Andrea Gritti who once governed the Venetian Republic, doesn't let you down either in service or style. His portrait, painted by Titian, hangs in one of the lounges as a silent reminder of Venice's most glorious era, the 16th century. It was a time of immense private fortunes, enough for Gritti to buy a stretch of sandbank near St Mark's Square as the site for a family home grand enough to welcome both local patricians and foreign aristocrats.

Though modern comforts have long since been added, the Venetian architecture — crenellated walls, mullioned windows, porticoes, stairways leading to courtyards where parapets surround wells — has remained intact. And today's guests, while not necessarily lordly and wealthy, are mannered enought to appreciate what is a refined and tranquil atmosphere.

It was the peaceful genteel ambience, the position — a stone's throw from St Mark's Cathedral, with foundations lapped by the waters of the Grand Canal, and the view across to the shimmering Salute Church — which attracted writers here even when Venice was past its zenith. Even before the Gritti became a hotel, John Ruskin, for example, rented the top floor (originally the servants' quarters) where he wrote much of his famous book *The Stones of Venice* in the middle of the last century.

At this time Venice was a province of the Austrian Empire and many scribes, musicians and intellectuals flocked here and stayed at the Gritti Palace. This continued in the period between the two world wars when the company managing the Grand Hotel (then the most luxurious) on the Grand Canal took over the Gritti as its annexe. Since only a narrow canal separated the two buildings, the company connected them with a covered bridge that was reminiscent of the Bridge of Sighs. The Gritti was then used as accommodation for the Grand's most discerning clientele.

In 1947, CIGA (the noted Italian hotel company) took over and it was under their management that Somerset Maugham and Ernest Hemingway became guests. The essence of today's hotel is actually quite succinctly summed up by Maugham who said: 'Here at the Gritti one never becomes just a number... here everyone keeps their identity.' Hemingway loved the hotel, usually occupying the suite 115/116; here he wrote his novel about Italy, *Over the River and into the Trees*.

One doesn't have to find Harry's Bar to indulge in an excellent *bellini* (champagne and peach juice) — for the head barman at the Gritti prepares a superb one, himself. And there is nowhere more atmospheric for dining in summer than the open air terrace, canal-side restaurant.

These days, at certain times during the year, the Gritti offers special short courses on cooking the Venetian way and on the history of art, to allow those interested to widen their knowledge of the city's restored monuments. But for swimming and other active sports, guests take a hotel launch to the Venice Lido. These same launches are the mode of transfer to and from the airport. As with sister hotel, the Danieli, parking is only available in Piazzale Roma.

With such a central position, it is easy to explore much of Venice on foot, from the hotel.

Campo S.M. Giglio 2467, 30124 Venezia, Italy ∅ Venice (041) 794611

99	(76 double, 13 single, 10 suites; all with en suite bathroom, air conditioning, colour TV and mini bar)	✻ ℘	Top quality romantic Beach and watersports at sister hotel, Venice Lido
🏨	Year round	♫	No
✕	Very elegant Italian	£/$	A

Villa Igiea Grand Hotel

Villa Igiea Grand Hotel is the kind of bougainvillaea-clad pile they no longer build. Designed by Ernesto Basile in 1898, it has become a famous and exclusive hotel.

The strange mixture of Norman architecture with Art Nouveau (or the Liberty style as they call it in Italy) works. The carving and the murals in the grand salons are in pristine condition though they are the originals. There's a great deal of marble around so it's not a place to stay for those embarrassed by opulence but in my opinion it's worth every penny.

Located near the centre of Palermo, Villa Igiea is a few minutes by car from the central train station and about a ¾ hour drive from Punta Raisi airport.

90142 Palermo, Salita Belmonte 43, Italy.
∅ (091) 543744

110	6 suites (all spacious with en suite bathroom, colour TV, mini bar and air conditioning)	✳	Relaxing in the grand fashion
🏨	Year round	🏊	Saltwater swimming pool, tennis court
✗	Mediterranean specialities	🎵	Piano music every evening in the American Bar. Disco
		£/$	A

Imperial Palace Hotel

There couldn't be much more of a contrast between Queen Elena of Savoy and Hitler's mistress, Eva Braun, yet both women have stayed within the auspicious portals of this hotel. Queen Elena loved it in summer as did the rest of European high society of that epoch. Eva Braun found herself a guest here during the last world war when German forces occupied it.

The old section of the Imperial Palace used to be a private villa, built in 1889 by the Costa family, Corsican aristocrats. In 1910 an extension was added for hotel purposes and a local Santa Margherita Ligure family managed the property for some years. A farther extension in 1910 brought it to its present size. One of the most famous dates in its history is 16 April 1922 when Russian and German politicians met here to sign the 'Treaty of Rapallo' — that second floor meeting room is still in use.

Though the hotel today is part of an Italian hotel chain, it remains quite splendid in décor and service. It has become sophisticated in keeping with its five star status: a piano bar, a private beach club, beauty treatments. But it remains the most inviting and prestigious hostelry on the Ligurian coast with a superb position overlooking the Gulf of Portofino.

Situated in its own lush park, the Imperial Palace is easily walkable from the railway station or accessible via the

Rapallo exit of the Genoa-Livorno superhighway. Genoa airport is a 45 minute drive away.

16038 Santa Margherita Ligure, Via Pagana 19, Italy.
✆ (0185) 288991

---

106 18 suites (all rooms with en suite bathroom, colour TV, mini bar and air conditioning)

🏨 Apr–Oct

✕ Ligurian specialities and local wines are featured on the menu in the Liberty Restaurant. Garden on the Sea is an informal grill restaurant facing the gulf, for lunches

✳ Romantically grand

🏊 At the Beach Club there's a private beach with solarium, reached through the park. Heated seawater swimming pool in panoramic position. Beach club sporting facilities, Jun to Sep include gym classes, swimming lessons, wind surfing, water skiing, boat hire. Massage, hydro massage and beauty treatments also available. Golf course and tennis courts only 2 km (1 mile) away

♫ The Art Nouveau Imperiale is a smart piano bar. Entertainment is also offered in the more casual Victory, an American bar on the beach. On occasions, live orchestra music for dancing

£/$ A

San Domenico Palace Hotel

Its position alone is hard to resist: the Greek Theatre to one side, Mount Etna the other, and below, the bay of Taormina. The monks certainly had the right idea, for this hotel was originally a monastery built by Catanese nobles in the 15th century. Dominican friar, Damiano Rosso, for example, from the Rosso di Altavilla family, gave all his worldly goods to the convent in 1430 — but there was a proviso, one which didn't come to light until 1866, the year when the State confiscated all church property.

In that year, the State representative duly arrived at the convent, ready to grab the keys from the last monk left (Brother Vincento) only to be shown the Rosso will (which is in fact inscribed on his tombstone). The will stated that the convent was to return to the Rosso heirs if the monks ever abandoned it — and so the Cerami princes left the building which was destined to become a hotel.

As its name might suggest, the atmosphere here is more one of a palace than a convent, though the original cloisters have been well preserved, and the conference centre has been constructed from the ruins of San Domenico's ancient church. The names of the famous who have stayed here are indelibly etched on the hotel guest book: Elena, duchess of Savoy signed it in 1922; Richard Strauss in 1923; Luigi Pirandello in 1928. On later pages are the signatures of King

Farouk and writers, Thomas Mann and John Steinbeck.

The world of the cinema is well represented besides: the flourishing hand of Marlene Dietrich and other film stars — Susan Hayward, Ingrid Bergman, Cary Grant, Audrey Hepburn and Sophia Loren. Hollywood magnate, Sam Spiegel, was only one to dine here on San Domenico's famous spaghetti. And director Michelangelo Antonioni chose the hotel to film part of *L'Avventura*. However, the Truman Suite, one of the most beautiful and decorated in splendid Chinese style, is not where the president stayed — only where he would have stayed had he come to Taormina!

As you would anticipate, this pillared palace contains some very fine pieces of furniture — just look in the bar, or the corridors. But, of course, there are modern luxuries — an outdoor heated pool with a panoramic view and, next to it, an American bar with summer restaurant for informal lunches. You can expect impeccable service in the main Bounganvillees, terraced restaurant, as you can at all times. That spaghetti may be more or less what you'd expect from a trattoria (more money for sure), but it is dished out with such style. No wonder, they call the San Domenico the 'Queen' of Sicilian hotels.

Surrounded by its own colourful garden, the hotel is an hour's drive from Catania airport and only a few minutes from Taormina-Giardini railway station.

98039 Taormina, Piazza S. Domenico 5, Italy.
⌀ (0942) 23701

117	(mostly double, including several suites, all with en suite bathroom, colour TV and refrigerator bar)	✳	Like a Mayfair bank in an even more glamorous and sunny setting
🏨	Year round	♀	Outdoor pool, nearby tennis and private beach with car service
✕	Predictably international		
		♫	Piano bar music and Sicilian mandolin group
		£/$	A

Villa San Michele

Designed by Michelangelo and classed among Italy's National Trust Monuments, this Tuscan villa has only recently been converted to a small luxury hotel. It takes its name from the 15th-century church dedicated to St Michael the Archangel which was enlarged towards the end of that century into what you see today. (The internal courtyard with the crest of the Davanzati family, attributed to Donatello, dates back to 1416.) Many of the works of art once housed in the monastery are these days in the churches and galleries of Florence.

The site on the hill of Fiesole, looking towards Florence, was such a beautiful one there was much ecclesiastical rivalry and intrigue to rule the establishment, but the Franciscans managed to retain possession until 1808 when they were suppressed by Napoléon. It was then that the name was first associated with that of Cipriani when a religious order led by Sister Nicoletta Cipriani lived here for a while.

At the beginning of this century, American financier Henry White Cannon bought San Michele, restored the gardens and put a roof over the 15th-century courtyard. After last war's damage, it was again restored by Lucien Tessier who decided it should be a hotel. Since then it has moved back into the hands of a Cipriani who commissioned Paris architect Gerard Gallet to recreate the interior in Florentine style.

Serenity reigns supreme here, by the pool with its panoramic view, in the gardens which slopes down to two solitary little chapels, past cypress and olive trees. Though the hotel is appointed in keeping with 16th-century style, 20th-century extras are included like the jacuzzis in every room. And exquisitely prepared meals are served indoors and in the open-air, arcaded Loggia.

Villa San Michele is 85 km (53 miles) from Pisa and offers regular luxury transport to the centre of Florence, a 15 minute drive.

Via di Doccia, 50014 Fiesole (Florence), Italy.
✆ **(055) 59451**

28	(including suites, all with en suite bathroom and private jacuzzi)	✳	Serene
		℘	Heated outdoor pool. Riding and tennis in the
🏨	mid Mar–mid Nov		nearby village of Cascie,
✕	Refined Italian		18-hole golf course at the Ugolino Golf Club
		♫	Piano bar
		£/$	A

Villa Sassi

Villa Sassi is a quiet retreat from modern pressures, a 17th-century country palace that has seen cardinals and counts inside its walls. It is only a small hotel but an immaculate one sitting on a hilltop above Turin, surrounded by 2 hectares (5 acres) of private park, sheltered by century-old trees.

As a stately residence it has become an equally stately but not fussily decorated hotel, enough of a gem to warrant its membership in Relais et Châteaux. The sweet life here is just that — no gyms and health club, but fresh air and flowers, no pool, but first class cuisine and excellent wines, for dining inside or on the terrace.

The villa has a country house appeal but is within close proximity of commercial Turin.

47 Strada Traforo del Pino, Turin 10132, Italy.
∅ (011) 89 05 56

18 (all with en suite bathroom)		✳	Quietly elegant
		℘	No, but tennis and swimming not far away and a golf course 20 km (12 miles)
🏨	Year round, except for August		
✗	Specialities include Tagliarini and risotto. Restaurant is closed on Sun		
		♫	No
		£/$	?

AUSTRIA

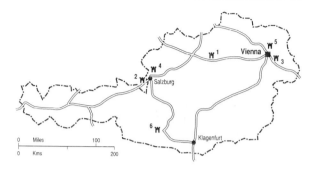

1   Hotel Schloss Dürnstein
2   Hotel Schloss Fuschl
3   Hotel Imperial
4   Hotel Schloss Monchstein
5   Hotel im Palais Schwarzenberg
6   Hotel Schloss Seefels

Austria boasts a large number of superb castles and palaces. Some, like Schönbrunn, are today showplace museums; some, like Palais Ferstel in Vienna, have become venues for international events. Others have become extremely fine hotels.

I have included one or two exceptional palace hotels with a truly historic legacy and one or two which were purpose-built in the palatial manner at the turn of the century, with many facilities. Admittedly there are more, but we'd like further personal reports before we feel they should be added.

One thing is assured — all of Austria's castle and palace hotels are in the top bracket. You can expect high quality of service and facilities, but be prepared to pay dearly for it. Austrian hospitality is generous, but not cheap. However, unlike many of the French and German châteaux, those in Austria are generally open year round.

Hotel Schloss Dürnstein

Situated in one of the loveliest stretches of the Danube valley, Schloss Dürnstein is a 17th-century romantic hideaway for lovers. True, this former residence of the Counts of Starhemberg is not exactly unknown — many a Wachau wine lover has imbibed a glass or two on its shaded terrace, has listened to a classical Chopin or Mozart melody. Many a celebrity from screen or political stage has sought solace within its solid walls. Poor Richard the Lion Heart came to know Durnstein quite well though not the flattering castle hotel service and stylish guest rooms — he was imprisoned in what is now the ruined fortress, a half hour's uphill walk away, in 1192, until England paid out a ransom in silver for his release.

King Leopold I may have enjoyed hospitality here, breaking his flight from the Turkish siege of Vienna in 1683, but he wouldn't have had the garden pool to immerse himself in, the sauna, the central heating, the super-soft beds and the goodnight sweets. He may, of course, have run into a prince or count or two — to be honest, one still can — but, providing one likes antiques, Persian carpets and gilded mirrors, the rest of us don't feel out of place either.

The castle overlooks the river with its barges and sightseeing boats. Its rooms are vaulted, its furnishings refined. Even the bar resembles a stately drawing room with cushioned stools and comfortable high-backed chairs. And if you have come to Austria for its food and wine (indeed, why not), the Schloss is the place. Its cellars contain all the wines that have made the Wachau area famous, including some from the castle's own vineyards. The kitchen presents hams and veal, quenelles and tortes to perfection.

The landscape is beautiful enough to have inspired painters to capture Wachau on canvas. There are good rambling routes and enough wine villages to keep the pace slow and leisurely. At harvest time, Durnstein houses display straw wreaths on their doors to show they have new wine for the pouring. The Schloss is located some 100 km (62 miles) from Vienna.

A-3601 Dürnstein, Austria. ✆ (02711) 212

35	(all tastefully decorated, all with private bathroom, TV and mini bar)	✳	Regal and stylish but not overbearing. Definitely for those who enjoy the good life
🏰	Apr–Oct		
✕	Gourmets delight in a candle-lit dining room with a Danube terrace. Specialities include pheasant stuffed with apricots, partridge, wild duck, fresh smoked trout, potato dumplings and Wachauer tortes. A cellar-full of Wachau wines, including those from the Schloss' own vineyard	℘	The hotel has its own sauna and an outdoor heated pool. The area is good for fishing and rambling
		♬	No
		£/$	A

Hotel Schloss Fuschl

Truly a regal and de luxe hotel in a superb setting, Schloss Fuschl was for many years the residence of Salzburg archbishops. It was built as a hunting lodge in 1450, the time that Michael Pacher carved his famous altar in neighbouring St Wolfgang. Its location, on a peninsula in Lake Fuschl, was a favourite hunting territory. Numerous festive events have been recorded such as the 'spectacular hunt' with 200 hounds held here in 1578 by Archbishop Baron Jakob Khuen, the 'festive hunt' of Prince Archbishop Wolf Dietrich von Raitenau in 1593. The greatest pomp and ceremony at Fuschl happened under the reign of Prince Archbishop Paris Count Lodron in the 17th century.

In 1833 it passed into private possession. (It was, for instance, German foreign minister Joachim von Rippentrop's residence in 1940.) But it was a subsequent owner, Carl Adolf Vogl, who turned the Schloss into a hotel when he acquired it in 1958. The guest book reveals both royal and star-status names: Prince Rainier, Queen Sikrit, Clark Gable, Richard Widmark — among them.

The castle conveys elements of its past extremely well: a warming open fireplace in the pillared vaulted hall suggests a genuine hunting lodge atmosphere — hunting may still be arranged around the lake. The swimming pool (part of the health club facilities) is dedicated to Diana, the goddess of hunting. And the whole of the hotel is furnished with antiques.

Traditional Austrian hospitality means not only living like a lord but dining like a king. Schloss Fuschl's tradition of haute cuisine is carried on in a choice of restaurants — for elegance, the Pink Salon; for a lakeside view, the Wintergarden and terrace. These and other public rooms are located in the Tower.

Guest accommodation is available in the Tower, Hunters Lodge, Guest House, Waldhaus and in the bungalows. All have views of either the lake or the 34-hectare (85-acre) park that surrounds the hotel and, as one might expect of a world-class hotel with an international clientele, are well equipped and furnished.

In such a romantic and peaceful location, it is easy enough to relax, drink in the scenery — but there are plenty of sporting possibilities on the hotel's own grounds. The Schloss has its own small golf course, tennis court and rifle range and is within proximity of plenty of other types of recreation. It is also home to one of Europe's exclusive beauty farms, The Lancaster, which offers spa and beauty programmes for men and women, either by single treatment, day or week long package. (Slimming diets are available if desired and fitness schedules include gym, sauna and massage.)

Located 30 km (19 miles) from Salzburg airport, Schloss Fuschl holds an excellent reputation for personalised service and princely comfort.

A-5322 Hof bei Salzburg, Austria. ✆ (06229) 253

90	(many suites; all with en suite bathroom, TV and mini bar)	✳ Rustic luxury
🏨	Year round	℗ First class. Schloss Fuschl has a 9-hole golf course, tennis court and private beach for boating, windsurfing, sailing. Also a bowling alley and private hunting preserve. Skiing and riding facilities nearby. Indoor pool, sauna and massage. Lancaster Beauty Farm
✗	Eat indoors or al fresco. Specialities include home-smoked char, river crab, quail and pheasant	
		♫ Music, from zither player to chamber music concerts
		£/$ A

Hotel Imperial

Once a princely palace, this exclusive Vienna hotel is still *the* regal place to stay. It was built for Duke Philipp of Württemberg and his bride, Maria Theresa, in 1865. She was the daughter of Archduke Albrecht (uncle of the Austrian Emperor and commanding officer of the Southern Army) and the marriage to a member of a southern German dynasty was hoped to bring about a permanent alliance against Prussia.

Munich architect, Arnold Zanetti, was commissioned to design a Renaissance-style palace on one of the roads crossing the elegant Ringstrasse. The coat of arms of the Württemberger family still adorns the hotel's façade.

When Vienna's hierarchy decided to build a road through the park that adjoined the palace, Duke Philipp lost interest in his residence and sold it to successful businessman, Franz Ritter von Landau — fully furnished. Now the splendid marble staircase, the balustrades and richly decorated pillars, the magnificent paintings and chandeliers became the setting for wealthy guests from around the world. In 1873 Palais Württemberg was converted into an exclusive hotel, opened by Kaiser Franz Joseph and renamed The Imperial.

It was only natural that a meeting place for monarchs and statesmen attracted others seeking prestige. Artists, scientists and representatives of industry stayed, among them Richard Wagner in 1875, in Vienna to supervise the first performance of 'Tannhauser' and 'Lohengrin'.

Even after 1918 when Austria had shrunk to a small Alpine republic, Vienna remained a mecca of the arts and good taste. John Galsworthy came, Thomas Mann and Luigi Pirandello.

Today, guests will find the hotel just as palatial. The reception rooms feature ceiling frescoes, valuable carpets and old masters, not to mention period furniture and artworks that are also antiques. The heavy red and gold Zur Majestat restaurant looks stately and the legendary Viennese coffee house atmosphere pervades Café Imperial. Guest rooms and suites in soft shades seem as royal as some of their former occupants but contain all the niceties of modern-day living.

Centrally situated as it is, the hotel is within easy walking distance of the State Opera House, St Stephan's Cathedral and the finest shops.

Karntner Ring 16, A-1015 Vienna, Austria.
✆ (0222) 65 17 65

162	(including suites; all with en suite bathroom, TV and mini bar)	✳	Turn of the century elegance
🏨	Year round	⅊	No
✕	Traditional Viennese and Austrian but prepared the lighter way. Prix fixe lunches and dinners as well as à la carte, also opera suppers	♫	Piano concerts and dinner music
		£/$	A

Hotel Schloss Monchstein

In Mozart's hometown of Salzburg, there is a mountain called Monchsberg rising directly from the centre — one of the loveliest spots on earth, according to explorer, Alexander von Humboldt. Crowning the top is a crenellated, ivy-clad castle hotel whose reputation for excellence has spread far and wide.

Schloss Monchstein was built in 1358 to house the guests of the archbishops. In 1622 it became an estate of the Monastery of Muelin (below the castle) and in 1654 it went to the estates of the University of Salzburg where it was used for R & R by tired professors. (Its nickname at the time was 'Professorenschloess'.)

Many a musical soirée took place at the castle in the 18th century — Mozart himself played here, and such illustrious guests as Alexander II's consort, Catherine of Russia, and Austria's Queen Elisabeth visited during the 19th century when the park was expanded. In 1887, Baron Leitner, a leading Salzburg banker, bought Monchstein and installed the first lift over the rocks on the outside of the mountain. today, guests use the efficient lift service to reach the old town in ten minutes. The same baron built a street going up the mountain as well as walking paths.

After Leitner's death in 1918, the castle was remodelled and, in 1948, converted into a hotel. Its position makes it particularly attractive, for while it is a haven of peace there on its mountain, the city is very accessible. Manicured lawns and gardens, embellished by statuary, lend a countrified air to what, after all, is an urban hotel.

There is an aristocratic charm about Monchstein. Individually designed rooms and suites, halls and public rooms are decorated with antiques from a number of different periods. One dines elegantly above the rooftops of Salzburg in the gourmet restaurant, Paris Lodron, which has won several awards for its cuisine. At other times of the day, food and refreshments are served in the Schlosssalon café or the garden terrace. The hotel looks after its guests with finesse, offering complimentary canapés with drinks and leaving goodnight sweets at bedtime.

Salzburg is one of Europe's most romantic and cultural cities, filled with landmarks and always a festival air. For relaxation at the hotel itself, there's a tennis court and walking paths all round.

Am Monchsberg 26, Salzburg 5020, Austria.
✆ (0662) 8413630

17	(8 doubles, 8 suites, 1 single, individually decorated; all with en suite bathroom and colour TV)	✳	Intimate, aristocratic elegance
		℘	Tennis court in grounds. Hiking paths in vicinity
🏛	Year round	♫	No
✗	Award-winning Austrian and international	£/$	A

Hotel im Palais Schwarzenberg

This superb baroque palace, set in an oasis of a park in the heart of Vienna, is still owned by a prince whose family have lived here since the 18th century.

The most luxurious rooms are the state rooms, these days used mostly for elite functions, though the whole hotel is furnished with antiques and objets d'art, chandeliers and fabric-covered walls. The most impressive room is the Marble Salon, maintained in its original form with paintings by Carre, Tamm, Hamilton, Horemans, Wouverman and Lingelbach, stucco reliefs by Johann and Balthasar Haggen-muller and a ceiling fresco by Gran.

This palace hotel is discreet and luxurious but certainly not cheap. Guest rooms in the former stables and servants' quarters are plush and most of them have a view of the park.

Schwarzenbergplatz 9, Vienna 1030, Austria.
✆ (0222) 784515

39	(including suites, individually styled; all with en suite bathroom)	✳	Stylish
		℘	Unheated outdoor pool, 5 tennis courts, sauna
🏨	Year round	♫	Piano music
✕	Traditional French and Austrian	£/$	A

Hotel Schloss Seefels

It may be difficult to decide whether this is a castle hotel or just a very plush, luxurious modern one. It is, in reality, both. Set on a rocky point above the lake the original core was built in 1860 and since then has been expanded, refined and glamorised.

For the person who wants it all, Seefels has it all, what with its waterfront and private beach with its own terrace restaurant; its beauty and medical centre; its tennis courts; its main dining room; and five star service.

Located a ten minute drive from Portschach, the hotel is surrounded by a park. Accommodation is in two wings joined by a castle corridor — all those in the west wing have a lakeside view, those in the east have lake or park view. As you would expect of a highly rated hotel, all furnished with up-to-date conveniences and comforts.

Children benefit at Seefels for there is a pool and playgrounds just for them and a supervised outdoor programme. In July, festival time, children's entertainment adds another excitement.

Airport transfers are available in the hotel's own limousines — Klagenfurt is the nearest, 17 km (10½ miles).

Toeschling 1, A-9210 Poertschach am Worther See, Austria. ✆ (04272) 2377

80 (all with en suite bathroom, TV and mini bar)

🏨 Year round

✗ Austrian and international

🎾 Indoor and outdoor pool, solarium, whirlpool, sauna, massage, medical baths, beauty treatments. Four tennis courts, private beach. Possibilities for boating, surfing, sailing, waterskiing. Space for deckchairs, sunshades and parasols. 18-hole golf course nearby. In winter, skiing in the vicinity

🎵 Drop In nightclub, hewn out of the rock, for disco music and party nights

£/$

PORTUGAL

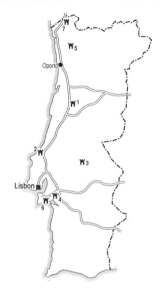

1 Palace Hotel do Buçaco
2 Estalgem do Convento
3 Pousada dos Loios
4 Pousada do Castelo de Palmela
5 Pousada de Santa Maria de Oliveira
6 Pousada de São Filipe
7 Pousada de São Teotónio

Though Portugal undoubtedly has its fair share of historic palaces, the country seems to have done less about them than some of its neighbours, certainly on any de luxe level. The most historic hotel conversions in Portugal to have earned world-wide recognition are, without doubt, the state-run pousadas — this country's equivalent to Spain's paradores. They are, in effect, inns, often located in scenic spots and sometimes incorporated into castles or convents of historic interest. Like the paradores, they tend to be simple rather than plush, with few facilities and a cuisine that is typical of the region.

An alternative to the pousadas are the estalagems which are also inns, but privately owned ones. They, too, are scattered throughout the country and some do have a great deal of character and atmosphere.

Palace Hotel do Buçaco

If there is a faded air about this palace hotel, as some reports suggest, at least it is exquisitely so, for who can resist the glamorous Manueline style and ornamentation of its public rooms, its luxuriant forest surrounds with their giant trees, lakes and gardens, and the peaceful air of the place.

The building as you see it now is 19th century but originally it was a Carmelite monastery in the 17th century — large but plain and simple, embellished by pebble mosaics. The monks also planted the forest — many of the trees still stand today, joined by more recent exotic varieties.

Towards the end of the 19th century, King Carlos, who had walked here as a child, agreed to the construction of a royal hunting lodge, a palace whose tower was to overlook the highest treetops. The work was entrusted to an Italian who built so close to the old monastery that he had to knock down the refectory, the infirmary and library to make space for the gallery of 12 archways, the rotunda whose pointed arches are lacy with openwork stone and public rooms are wide as esplanades.

There was a British connection with Buçaco before it was ever a hotel — look at the gnarled tree near the entrance and you'll see the sign: Wellington's olive tree. For the Iron Duke spent a week in one of the monk's cells prior to the Battle of Buçaco.

The first hotel guests at the turn of this century marvelled at the richness and comfort of large and airy rooms with bathrooms, pitch pine furniture, bevelled mirrors and brass beds, and electricity! Buçaco became fashionable.

The hotel is located 29 km (18 miles) from Coimbra, a handsome university town, only 4 km (2½ miles) from Luso and very near a number of vineyards.

Floresta do Buçaco, Buçaco 3050, Aveiro, Portugal.
✆ **(032) 93101**

60	(including suites; all with en suite bathroom)	✳	Old fashioned grandeur
🏨	Year round	⚲	Tennis courts. Plenty of grounds and forest for nature walks
✕	Portuguese and international		
		♫	No
		£/$	C

Estalgem do Convento

An 'estalegem' is an inn and a stay at this one is more than appropriate to a visit to the medieval walled town of Óbidos, a picturesque maze of cobbled alleys and piazzas. The inn, which stands on the outskirts of the wall, was to have been a convent for, in 1830, the prior of St Peter's, Antonio Goncalves d'Asseca, sought to found a nunnery here. Like all parishes, he was short of cash and had to ask the district's wealthy to lend a hand. The funds were still insufficient but luckily King Miguel was visiting Óbidos, granted the prior's request and the building of the cloister was begun in 1831.

Since then, the cloister has seen several owners until a French family turned it into an inn. Today it belongs to a local family who offer guests a glimpse of the past in a comfortable way. The hotel is ideal for those who prefer character to chic chintz.

Rua Dom Joaõ de Omelas, Óbidos 2510, Leiria, Portugal. ✆ (062) 95217

27	(21 doubles, 6 suites; all with en suite bathroom; suites have TV)	✳	Portuguese olde worlde
		℘	No
		♫	No
🏨	Year round	£/$	C
✕	Portuguese and international		

Pousada do Castelo de Palmela

A transformed convent inside a 1000-year-old castle, surrounded by fortified walls, this pousada stands above the pretty white-walled town of Palmela. The convent was built in 1423 by the order of King Joaõ I and became the headquarters for the Order of Santiago by royal decree in 1443.

For a pousada, this one is furnished quite lavishly and reports consider the staff helpful and the food above average. From the windows you can see the surrounding plains and olive groves and, in the distance, the coast. An impressive cloister area borders the traditional courtyard filled with plants and is generally used as a lounge area. Setúbal is 7 km (4 miles) away.

Palmela 2950, Setúbal, Portugal. ✆ **(01) 235 12 26**

27	(double, including suites; all with en suite bathroom)	✳ Blend of past and present
🏨	Year round	℘ Large grounds with heated pool and children's play area. Nearby sandy beaches. river for fishing and sailing 7 km (4 miles)
✗	Good standard	
		♫ No
		£/$ C

Pousada de Santa Maria de Oliveira

Portugal's first king was born in Guimarães, a town at the foot of the Sierra Santa Catarina, in the heart of Minho province. The pousada, a conversion of noble manor houses, is situated right in the historic centre of town, in the cathedral square, and is the perfect base from which to explore the beauties of Portugal's most fertile and green province.

Like all pousadas, this one is simply furnished but adequately comfortable, with two bars, garden and terrace. It is friendly, featuring much of the local linen and regional cuisine. Good value for money.

Apartado 101, Guimarães, 4800 Braga, Portugal.
✆ (053) 41 21 57

16	(mostly double, including suites, all with private bathroom)	✳	Attentive and friendly
		℘	No
🏨	Year round	♫	No
✗	Plentiful and typical of Portugal	£/$	C

Pousada de São Filipe

Pousadas are to Portugal what paradores are to Spain, many with historical connections — and this one is no exception. Built on the site of a 16th-century fort, it perches above the port of Setúbal overlooking the bay and fishing fleet.

São Filipe became a pousada in 1965, but its military air has been softened. The dining room is quiet — whitewashed walls, wooden ceiling, crisp linen cloths — the setting for à la carte or fixed price menus. Equally simple, but comfortable, the bedrooms are adequately furnished.

Do look at the pousada's chapel — you don't have to arrange a marriage there to admire the decorative tiles that represent the life of the fortress' patron saint, São Filipe — a work carried out by Policarpo de Oliveira in 1736.

Pousada de São Filipe is located an hour's drive from Lisbon, 1 km (½ mile) west of Portugal's fourth largest city, Setúbal.

Setúbal 2900, Portugal. ☎ (065) 23844

15	(mostly double, some with private bath or shower)	✳	Simple, tasteful but prices may seem somewhat steep
🏨	Year round	♪	No
✗	Basically fish dishes in pleasant restaurant	♫	No
		£/$	C

Readers who are anxious to sleep in a Napoleonic bed or study a cannon-shelled wall in their historic hostelry will say that the Pousada de São Teotónio looks purpose built, not at all their idea of ancient splendour. Well, it is true it opened as a hotel in 1962 but it was built on the 17th-century ramparts of a Vaubanesque frontier fortress with a marvellous view of the Minho River and the Spanish city of Túy.

The Minho valley is a delightfully peaceful section of Portugal to explore — not to mention its vinho verdes (green wines) which are so palatable and so inexpensive. Valença's fortress had become one of the country's greatest strongholds by the end of the 17th century and today within those walls you will find a charged atmosphere. Narrow, pebbled winding streets, tunnels and arches, monuments like the 12th-century former Parish Church of Santa Maria dos Anos.

4930 Valença do Minho, Portugal. ✆ (051) 222 52

16	(all double with en suite bathroom)	✳	Cheerful
🏨	Year round	♀	No, but river and sea fishing nearby
✗	River salmon and broa (cornmeal bread)	♫	No
		£/$	C

European Extras

The rest of Europe has not been quick to seize the opportunities that hotel conversions could offer, or have preferred to keep their palaces either as royal residences or as museum showplaces as in Scandinavia, where hotel influences have been of the modern or rustic variety.

You will, of course, find 'palatial' styled hotels in European capitals like Stockholm and even Bucharest and the Budapest Hilton incorporates a segment of an old castle, but they do belong to a different category than the type of accommodation mentioned in this book. I do admit to including a couple of Swiss purpose-built palace hotels because they are so famous, and point out that Turkey has tried conversions with two hotels in Istanbul.

Neither Belgium nor Holland are noted for castles, although there is one entry for the latter, which also boasts some fine hotel conversions from merchants' houses. Luxembourg has its share of castles but these are mainly 'sights' or under private ownership. We continue, however, to look for more of the authentic, so further suggestions would be welcomed.

Château Gütsch

The word 'Gütsch' means peak or head, top — and that's where this strangely turreted, exclusive hotel is located — on top of a wooded hill above Lucerne. It even has its own private funicular to reach the city (though there's road access as well).

Gütsch is not a castle in the true sense of the word — one of the former owners bestowed the title 'château' because of its many towers and fancy façade. The hotel has never pretended to have had royal or titled owners but it does feature antiques and paintings in keeping with its grand name.

Candle-light, dinner dances, a cosy cellar bar, attentive friendly Swiss service are the plus factors.

Kanonenstrasse, CH-6002, Lucerne, Switzerland.
✆ (041) 2202

40	(mostly double, including suites and four posters, all with en suite bathroom)	✳	Romantic
		℘	Outdoor heated pool
🏨	Year round	♫	Dinner dances with live
✕	International for the elitist		music. Also live music in
			the bar
		£/$	B

Lausanne Palace

The Lausanne Palace is, I admit, one of my 'cheats' because although it has certainly hosted royalty, it was never owned by those of royal blood. Instead, it was built to be what it is — a grand luxury hotel. But palatial in style, in looks it is, built at the turn of the century when grand hotels were spacious and opulent, and could afford to be.

Whether Swiss hotels like this one created the country's fine reputation for hoteliering is a question I wouldn't care to comment on, but the esteem in which the rest of the world and the hotel industry holds Switzerland is a fact — and a stay in this hotel will show you why.

It is located in the heart of the city with a magnificent view over Lake Geneva and the Alps, yet a few minutes' walk from the best shopping streets and the charming old quarter. It may not boast of historic deeds and legends, but its pillared and chandeliered public rooms are full of haute grandeur. Comfort besides.

Both its restaurants are terraced, facing the lake. Gourmets (be they overnight guests or not) will tell you that Le Relais is one of the best places to dine in Lausanne, and its bar one of the most refined. Service is no less in La Verandah whose menu indicates light meals and French specialities. Being a hotel of renowned international standing, it has its own nightclub and two cinemas; a sauna and relaxation centre; boutiques and sport facilities within its vicinity.

Located three minutes from the railway station and 60 km (37 miles) from Geneva's airport.

7–9 Grand-Chene, 1002 Lausanne, Switzerland.
✆ (021) 20 37 11

167 (many suites; all with en suite bathroom, TV and mini bar)

🏨 Year round

✕ Gourmet dishes in the elegant setting of Le Relais. La Veranda for light meals and French specialities. Breakfast, light snacks and afternoon tea are served in the 'Hall du Palace'

✳ Calm and gracious — the best of Swiss hospitality

🎾 Sauna, massage and relaxation centre on the premises. In the vicinity are watersports, tennis, an 18-hole golf course, swimming pools, riding. Skiing and skating are possible in winter some 45 minutes' drive away.

🎵 Afternoon piano music. Two cinemas within the hotel and a nightclub featuring an international show

£/$ A

Montreux Palace

This gem of Art Nouveau architecture was, like other Swiss counterparts, built to be a hotel, but in the palatial manner demanded around the beginning of the 20th century. Montreux was only a collection of villages until the late 19th century when development boomed; with the building of the railways, tourists had access to wonderul panoramas and wanted somewhere wonderful to stay. Montreux Palace achieved that in 1905, with its vast halls, grand staircases and terraces, and a sumptuous banqueting hall that was to become *the* venue for High Society. Endless mirrors and sculpted columns were the order of the day. They still are. Plaster nymphs still decorate the walls even if portions of the hotel have been modernised, and bedrooms and marbled bathrooms are extravagantly large.

Located 80 km (50 miles) from the airport.

100, Grand Rue, CH 1820 Montreux, Switzerland.
✆ **(021) 963 53 73**

190	(including 40 suites; all with en suite bathroom, TV, balcony)	✳	Attentive luxury
🏨	Year round	℘	Indoor fitness centre with sauna and solarium. Outdoor heated pool and all-weather tennis court.
✕	Outstanding French food in Restaurant Français; Swiss specialities in La Cave du Cygne.	♫	Musical entertainment in the bars
		£/$	A

Hotell Refsnes Gods

Hotell Refsnes Gods never was a castle (though it was built up around a handsome country mansion) but it looks like one and indeed is a member of the prestigious French-based Relais et Châteaux consortium. Hospitality, on the other hand, has been its hallmark for 200 years since it was the centre for society in the 1770s.

The estate itself was under the control of the Oslo Bishopric in 1400 and still belonged to the church in 1593 with sawmills and cornmills on the Moss River. From the Church it passed into private hands, reaching local merchant, David Chrystie, in 1749. He loved Refsnes, planted the famous lime tree avenue in front of the house and kept the grounds well tended. The Chrysties were ardent entertainers, hosting dinners and balls for top society at their hunting lodge, as Refsnes was referred to.

David Chrystie was not the only one to fall in love with this wonderful estate — when his family ownership ended after 50 years, it passed to another who loved it just as much — Consul Loretz Meyer, who made the purchase in 1855. No, he didn't give parties like his predecessors, but he did admire their trees and returned here each and every summer with friends and family, until his death in 1888. He enlarged the house and extended the grounds. And he did invite the noteworthy of his time, as did his daughter when the estate passed to her. Ibsen couldn't/wouldn't allow the temptation to interrupt his work in the 1890s, when he was writing 'Little Eyolf', but King Oscar certainly turned up for a dinner in his honour in 1898.

Refsnes has never been neglected and hardly ever empty. Before it was ever a hotel, it was a restaurant, though perhaps it was restaurateurs Armand and Bjørn Christiansen who put that restaurant on the 'eating' map when they took over the house in 1955. Even once the hotel wing was added in 1971 and another sale processed in 1986, the Christiansen family continues to be responsible for the management of what is now a luxury hotel.

These days, the guest rooms are in the newly built wings, overlooking the fjord or swimming pool, while the old house itself has been converted to the reception, bar, restaurant and function room area. No one would refute the comfort. One split-level lounge overlooks the pool; the other, velvety and equally welcoming has a bar area; bedrooms are sizeable and modern. The pool, sauna and bathing beach are available for guests' use, but Refsnes Gods doesn't feature an 'activities schedule'.

Located in a quiet residential area on Jeløy, one of the largest islands along the east coast of Oslofjord and linked to the mainland by bridge, the hotel is 3 km (2 miles) from the small town of Moss, 60 km (37 miles) south of Oslo. The green and leafy island of Jeløy allows both maize and vines to grow and the area within the immediate neighbourhood of the hotel is good for walking. (On the cultural side, one of Norway's best art galleries is 1½ km (1 mile) away.)

Godset 5, Jeløy 1501, Moss, Norway. ✆ **(032) 70411**

62	(33 single, 25 double, 4 suites; all with en suite bathroom, TV and mini bar)	✳	Elegant international
		♇	Heated outdoor pool, sauna, private bathing beach and marina. Golf and tennis facilities (under way at time of writing)
🏠	Year round, except Christmas and Easter		
✗	Continental and Norwegian. High Relais standards of cuisine	♫	No
		£/$	B

Pera Palace

Pera Palace was built to welcome and refresh arriving visitors off the Orient-Express when it started service to Istanbul in 1892. Lavishly decorated with marble and hand-made Turkish carpets and other works of art, it became the fashionable meeting place for the royal and titled heads of state as well as famous film stars. Room 101 which was once occupied by Atatürk is now reserved as a museum piece. Other famous guests have included Edward VIII, Mata Hari and Jackie Kennedy. And where did Agatha Christie disappear to but here — an impressive grand salon is named for her.

This four star city hotel is the type they can't afford to build any more, retaining its air of mystery and nostalgia that are so associated with Istanbul itself.

Mesrutiyet Cad. 98, Tepebasi, Istanbul, Turkey.
☎ 1514560

120	(including suites; all with private bathroom)	✳	Faded grandeur
		℘	No
🏨	Year round	♫	No
✕	Turkish and international	£/$	

Hotel Grad Otocec

A honey-stoned castle in Yugoslavia? Yes it does exist, and by that country's standards is quite grand (though it is categorised 'B'). It dates back to the 13th century and has known many a feudal master including Count Ivan Lenkovic, general of the Military Border.

Located on an island in the river Krka whose banks either side may be reached by wooden bridges, this hotel is surrounded by pleasant greenery and is the key attraction of a tourist complex which includes a large modern hotel, motel, self-catering bungalows and camping facilities.

Scrupulously well-scrubbed as Yugoslav hotels tend to be, Grad Otocec mixes wooden ceilings with tiled floors, features an outdoor terrace and period furniture in at least two suites. Restaurant service can be slow but the food is good value for money.

Otocec Ob Krki 68222, Yugoslavia. ✆ (068) 21830

21 (mostly double, including suites; all with private bathroom)	✳ More charm than expected
	⚲ River for bathing, boating and fishing. Horse riding with or without a trainer
🏨 Year round	
✕ Local and international cuisine	♫ Dinner dance at Restaurant Otocec
	£/$ C

Kasteel Wittem

Situated in the Geul Valley, Wittem Castle has been a citadel for centuries. In the 13th century it came into the possession of the Knights of Julemont who called themselves van Wittem and resided here until a descendant sold it for 300 guilders in 1344. The new owner, Jan van Cosselaer, assumed the van Wittem name. In 1520 Emperor Charles V made Wittem a Barony. During the Eighty Years War, the first Prince of Orange conquered the castle from the Spaniards. After that war, compensation money paid for Wittem's restoration and enlargement, and the Counts of Waldeck moved in.

After several other ownerships, Wittem became a hotel in 1958. These days, aperitifs are served on the terrace by the moat and, in addition to the van Pallant Hall Restaurant, an à la carte dining room is available in the Prince Hall. Award-winning cuisine is served in both.

Kasteel Wittem is located between Maastricht (17 km, 10½ miles) and Aachen (15 km, 9 miles).

Wittemerallee 3, Limberg 6286 AA, Holland.
✆ (04450) 1208

12	(all with en suite bathroom)	✳	Refined simplicity
		♂	No, but tennis, fishing, golf
	Year round		nearby
✗	High quality, Michelin-rosetted	♫	No
		£/$	B